ESSENTIALS OF

WINDOWS™ 3.1

by PicTorial

PicTorial Series

Dennis P. Curtin, Series Editor

ESSENTIALS OF
WINDOWS™ 3.1
by PICTORIAL

Dennis P. Curtin

Prentice Hall Career & Technology
Englewood Cliffs, New Jersey 07632

Library of Congess Cataloging-in-Publication Data

Curtin, Dennis P.
    Essentials of Windows 3.1 by PicTorial / Dennis P. Curtin.
    p.   cm.—(PicTorial series)
    Includes index.
    ISBN 0-13-294589-4 (pbk)
    1. Windows (Computer programs)   2. Microsoft Windows (Computer programs)
I. Title. II. Series: Curtin, Dennis P., PicTorial series.
QA76.76.W56C867   1994
005.4'3—dc20   93-37137
                                        CIP

Windows is a trademark of Microsoft Corporation.

Acquisitions editor: Liz Kendall
Production editor: Cecil Yarbrough
Creative director: Paula Maylahn
Electronic production and design: Function Thru Form, Inc.
Project manager at Function Thru Form: Gwen Waldron
Art director and interior designer: Robin D'Amato
Icon design: Clea Chmela
Illustrations: Freddy Flake
Zoom art: Rita Myers
Cover design: Marianne Frasco
Cover art: © David Bishop/Phototake NYC
Manufacturing buyer: Ed O'Dougherty
Supplements editor: Cindy Harford
Editorial assistant: Jane Avery

© 1994 by Prentice Hall Career & Technology
Prentice-Hall, Inc.
A Paramount Communications Company
Englewood Cliffs, NJ 07632

Printed in the United States of America
10 9 8 7 6 5 4 3 2

ISBN 0-13-294589-4

Prentice-Hall International (UK) Limited, *London*
Prentice-Hall of Australia Pty, Limited, *Sydney*
Prentice-Hall of Canada Inc., *Toronto*
Prentice-Hall Hispanoamericana, S.A., *Mexico*
Prentice-Hall of India Private Limited, *New Delhi*
Prentice-Hall of Japan, Inc., *Tokyo*
Simon & Schuster Asia Ptd. Ltd., *Singapore*
Editora Prentice-Hall do Brasil, Ltda., *Rio de Janeiro*

CONTENTS

PREFACE

When IBM PCs were first introduced in the early 80s, they used an operating system called DOS (which stands for "Disk Operating System"). Most IBM PCs and the millions of similar computers that have been sold continue to use this operating system. When using DOS, you enter a command by typing it in. DOS has hundreds of commands, and it can be a fairly demanding task to remember the ones you need. As computers have become faster and more powerful, it has become possible to take a lot of the difficulty out of computing by designing interfaces, or screen displays, that are not only attractive but also easy to use. These new interfaces, which make extensive use of icons (little graphical pictures) and menus (lists of commands), are called graphical user interfaces (GUI—pronounced "goo-ey"—for short). There are a number of graphical user interfaces in use today, and Windows is by far the most popular.

Windows has three immediately noticeable features. First, its graphic screen contains many icons that you can click to operate programs and execute commands. Second, it displays commands on menus so you can choose the one you want without having to remember how to type it in. Finally, it can run more than one program at a time. This is very useful, especially when you want to transfer data from one program to another. Windows also has one feature that isn't so obvious. It still uses the DOS operating system but hides it unless you want to find it.

This text introduces you to Windows without assuming that you have prior computing experience. Everything you need to know to become a proficient Windows user is presented here. You needn't bring anything else to your learning experience except a willingness to explore a new and exciting way to compute.

■ ORGANIZATION

This text is organized into chapters, which in turn are organized into pictorial tutorials called *PicTorials*. Each PicTorial begins with objectives and then proceeds step by step through a series of related procedures. The concept behind each procedure is first discussed, and then a *tutorial* guides you in exploring the concept on the computer. At the end of each PicTorial are a number of *skill-building exercises* that you use to practice the procedures that you have learned at the computer. Following the exercises is a *visual quiz* that tests your understanding of the elements you have explored in the PicTorial.

Chapter 1 covers Program Manager—how you use it to open, close, size, and drag windows and execute commands.

Chapter 2 introduces File Manager and shows you how to use it to manage disks, files, and directories.

Chapter 3 uses Windows' built-in Notepad application to teach you basic Windows procedures such as opening and saving files, printing files, and cutting and pasting. Notepad is so easy to use that it doesn't get in the way of your learning. You are then introduced to running non-Windows applications from within the Windows environment. In this section you will see how you use programs such as WordPerfect for DOS and 1-2-3 for DOS side by side with Windows applications such as WordPerfect for Windows and Excel for Windows.

■ KEY FEATURES

Windows is a visually oriented program, so this text uses a visual approach. It features two unique elements, PicTorials and VIsual Quizzes, in addition to a number of other features designed to make it a better learning tool.

Common Wrong Turns boxes alert you to where many people make mistakes and show you how to avoid them.

Tips boxes point out shortcuts and other interesting features about many procedures.

Looking Back boxes are used whenever a procedure that has been discussed earlier is essential to completing a new task. These summaries are intended to remind you how to perform a task without your having to refer back in the text.

Looking Ahead boxes are used whenever a procedure is unavoidably referred to before it has been discussed in detail. These boxes help you avoid confusion by providing a brief description and an assurance that a more detailed discussion will follow.

Pausing for Practice boxes appear periodically in tutorials when essential procedures have been introduced. They encourage you to stop at key points and practice these procedures until they become second nature.

PICTORIAL FEATURES

▶ *PicTorials* are heavily illustrated tutorials. The visuals serve two purposes. First, they help explain concepts. Second, they tell you when you are on course as you follow the steps in the tutorials.

▶ *VISual Quizzes* at the end of each PicTorial test your understanding of the Windows environment. Unlike standard questions presented in just words, these questions are illustrated.

▶ Five different kinds of *boxes* help make the book easy to use.

CHAPTER FEATURES

▶ At the end of each chapter you will find a wide variety of true-false, multiple choice, and fill-in-the-blank questions to test how well you have understood the material.

▶ *Projects* at the end of every chapter give you the opportunity to practice the procedures you have learned in that chapter and demonstrate that you have mastered them.

SUPPLEMENTS

The following supplements to this text have been made available by the publisher:

▶ The *Windows Student Resource Disk*. This disk contains all of the files needed to complete the computer activities in this text. A master disk can be duplicated for students.

▶ An *Instructor's Manual with Tests*, prepared by Donna Matherly of Tallahassee Community College. The manual contains suggested course outlines for a variety of course lengths and formats, teaching tips and a list of competencies to be attained for each PicTorial, solutions and answers to VISual Quizzes and all computer activities, and a complete test bank of over 200 questions.

▶ A *Windows Instructor's Resource Disk*. This disk features an important file created by Gray Patton of Forsyth Technical Community College, designed to be installed on your systems and help you and your students get more enjoyment from the course. This is a batch file that restores Windows to the way it was when it was first installed. Any settings changed by students and any icons or groups that have been deleted are automatically restored. Automatically restoring all settings should prove to be a great timesaver for the lab manager. And much instructor time should be saved because many unnecessary questions caused by system changes left over from previous users will be eliminated.

◼ THE PICTORIAL SERIES

This text is part of the PicTorial Series, an innovative series of highly visual Windows applications books. This book is an abridged version of *Windows™ 3.1 by PicTorial*. Instructors who are looking for more extensive coverage of Windows 3.1 will find it in the longer text. Contact your local Prentice Hall representative for a complete listing of books available in this series.

◼ NOTES TO THE INSTRUCTOR

▶ When working with Windows, you can execute most commands by just pointing and clicking with the mouse. In most cases there are also alternate keyboard commands that you can use. Except where the alternate keyboard commands are obviously superior, this text discusses only the mouse commands, and the computer activities assume that computers are equipped with a mouse.

▶ The PicTorials in this text are based on the default Windows screen display that appears when you first install the program. They assume that the

StartUp and Applications group windows may vary but otherwise that your systems will be set up so they look like the illustration in PicTorial 1's section "Exploring the Windows Screen."

▶ When students work with Windows, they can make changes in it that affect the next user. If these changes remain in effect, some of the hands-on activities in this text will not work as described. To overcome this problem, the *Windows Instructor's Resource Disk* contains a batch file that copies all of the important Windows files (*.ini* and *.grp)* to a hidden directory on drive C. Then each time Windows is loaded, these files are automatically copied to the Windows directory, where they ensure that the program runs as originally installed. If you make any changes to Windows that you want to preserve, you can run the *install* portion of this batch file system, and it copies the changed files to the hidden directory so they are preserved.

■ ACKNOWLEDGMENTS

Working on this text has been an unusually enjoyable experience. No book is ever the work of a single individual, so teams of people assemble to get the job done and then disperse to other jobs when they have finished. The development of this text has drawn together the most talented and committed group of people that I have ever had the experience of working with. Here they are, in the order in which they became involved in the project.

To begin, David Ford worked with the author during the development of the text's concept. The book's heavily visual approach required the insights of a designer such as David who could work with the author on how best to integrate text and graphics to the extent done here. At the publisher's end have been Liz Kendall and Cecil Yarbrough, both of whom have made major contributions to the text from beginning to end. On the academic end have been the reviewers and contributors who have tried to make this the best possible text. They include the following:

> Cheryl L. Dukarich, Pima Community College
>
> Sandra S. Hagman, Forsyth Technical Community College
>
> Norman P. Hahn, Thomas Nelson Community College
>
> Sue Higgins, Community College of Rhode Island
>
> Sally L. Kurz, Coastline Community College
>
> Amelia J. Maretka, Wharton County Junior College
>
> Gray Patton, Forsyth Technical Community College
>
> Philip J. Sciame, Dominican College
>
> Betsy Walsh, Laney College

Finally, at the production end, thanks go to all of the people at Function Thru Form, who used the latest digital tools to take the book from raw manuscript to final published form as easily as it could be done (which is not the same as saying it was easy!). The people at Function Thru Form who contributed to the text include Clea Chmela, Robin D'Amato, Anne DeMarinis, Nelson Gomez, Keith James, Rita Myers, Lise Prawn, and Gwen Waldron. Supporting the production of the text were Freddy Flake, who prepared the dozens of line drawings, and Cathy Morin, who prepared over 700 images of the screen; Jane Avery, who coordinated reviewing; and Karen Moreau, the Prentice Hall representative in northern Florida who had some valuable suggestions for the author (as usual) which appear in this text as Common Wrong Turns boxes.

All of these people, each and every one, took a personal interest in this text; and that interest shows in the work you are now holding. Any shortcomings are of course the responsibility of the author (me) and in no way reflect on the professionalism and talent of this fine group.

About the Author

Dennis Curtin's 25-plus years' business experience in educational publishing provide a rich and unique perspective for his computer applications texts. He has served in executive positions at several companies, including Prentice Hall, where he has been a textbook sales representative, an acquisitions editor, editorial director of the engineering, vocational, and technical division, and editor in chief of the international division. For the past 9 years, he has been primarily a writer of college textbooks on end user computer applications.

Dennis has been involved with microcomputers since the introduction of the original Apple II. He was a beta tester for the first version of Lotus 1-2-3 when Lotus Corporation had only 9 employees squeezed into a small Kendall Square office. In the years since, he has taught in adult education and corporate training programs, but he readily acknowledges that he has learned most of what he knows about textbooks by working with thousands of instructors during the writing, reviewing, and revising of his own books.

The primary author and series editor of the COMPASS Series and author of several popular microcomputer concepts texts, he is now spearheading and developing an exciting new series of highly visual Windows applications texts called the PicTorial Series. This title is the first book in the PicTorial Series.

Dennis welcomes feedback and suggestions from students and instructors using his books. You can write to him at the following address:

Dennis Curtin
c/o Software Skills Editor
Prentice Hall College Division
113 Sylvan Ave, Rt. 9W
Englewood Cliffs, NJ 07632

ESSENTIALS OF

WINDOWS™ 3.1

by PicTorial

Chapter 1
WORKING WITH PROGRAM MANAGER

PICTORIAL 1

PROGRAM MANAGER –
AN INTRODUCTION

After completing this PicTorial, you will be able to:

▶ Start your computer system and load Windows

▶ Name and describe the parts of a window

▶ Point with the mouse

▶ Click and double-click the mouse

▶ Minimize, maximize, and restore windows

▶ Change the active window

▶ Drag windows and change their size

▶ Exit Windows and turn off your equipment

The microcomputer is a versatile machine. With it you can calculate a budget for this year's college expenses, plot a graph of the results, and, finding that you won't have enough money, write a letter to your boss asking for a raise. Each of these tasks is an *application*. To perform it, you load an *application program* specific to the task. For example, WordPerfect® and Microsoft® Word are word processing application programs used to enter, edit, and format memos, letters, reports, and other documents. Excel and 1-2-3® are spreadsheet application programs used to work with numbers and make calculations.

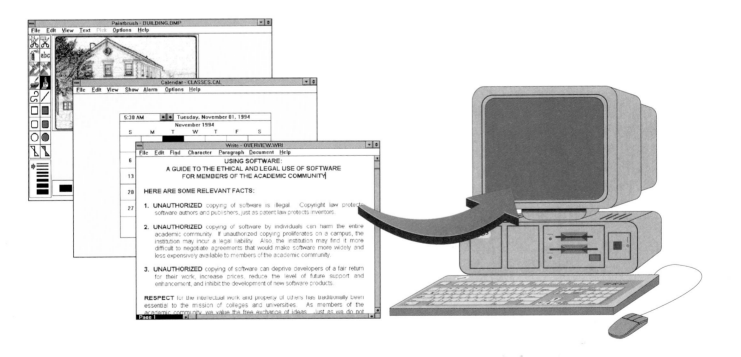

To change from one application to another you switch from one application program to another. In this sense, the computer is like an actor, and the application programs are like scripts. When the actor changes scripts, he or she can perform a different role. By changing application programs, you can make your computer perform different applications. Being *computer literate* means that you understand how to use application programs to perform useful work.

Windows is designed to make it easy to work with application programs. Unlike earlier systems where the screen just displayed a prompt such as C:\>, and you had to type commands, Windows' *Graphical User Interface* (also called a GUI—pronounced "goo-ee") allows you to choose commands from pull-down menus and run more than one application program at a time, each in its own window. Using Windows you can run a spreadsheet in one window and a word processor in another. Windows also gives a common look to most programs that are developed to take advantage of its features. Standard commands load programs; call up help; save, retrieve, and print files; enter and edit data; and quit applications. This makes it easier to learn new programs because many of your existing skills are transferable.

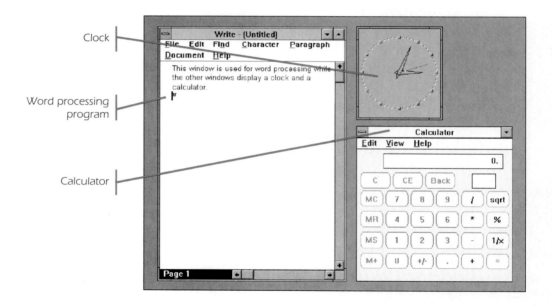

Clock

Word processing program

Calculator

The most important Windows application program is *Program Manager*. Program Manager is important because, unlike most other applications, it remains in the computer's memory from the time you load Windows until you quit. Program Manager's sole task is to start or *launch* all other Windows application programs such as word processors, spreadsheets, and database managers. When you exit an application that you launched from Program Manager, you always return to Program Manager.

This PicTorial introduces you to Program Manager step by step. All of the procedures you learn here will also apply to other Windows applications. They are fundamental to operating Windows, so take your time. The concepts and procedures that are introduced later will be much easier if you have mastered the procedures presented here.

LOADING WINDOWS

To use Windows, you begin by loading the computer's operating system, usually DOS. This is called *booting the system*. The term *booting* comes from the expression "pulling yourself up by your bootstraps."

COMMON WRONG TURNS: ANXIETY

If you have never before worked with a computer, now's the time to *relax*. New computer users often have anxieties about things that might go wrong. These fears, all of which are unjustified, include the fear they will somehow cause damage to the computer. There is nothing you can do to blow up the computer or otherwise hurt the system, so there is no reason to be anxious. Also, don't be intimidated by others who seem to grasp the procedures more quickly. They may have had previous experience with computers or just have a knack at these things. These differences among users tend to level out after a few weeks when everyone feels comfortable.

▶▶ TUTORIAL

1. Open the door to floppy drive A or eject any disk from that drive. When you turn on a computer, it looks to the *startup drive* for the operating system files that it needs to start up. On a hard disk system like the one you are using, the startup drive is the hard drive C, but the computer still looks to the floppy drive A first. If there is a disk in that drive when you turn on the computer, you could have a problem loading Windows.

2. To boot most systems, you just turn on the computer and the display monitor. If you can't find the on/off switches, ask someone where they are.

When you turn on the computer, it may seem to be inactive for a few moments. In fact, it is running a diagnostic program to be sure the system is operating correctly. What then happens and what you do next depends on how your system is set up. Windows may be loaded automatically or one of the other possible outcomes illustrated in the box "Things That Can Happen When You Boot a System" may occur.

The Windows screen display may appear when you boot your system.

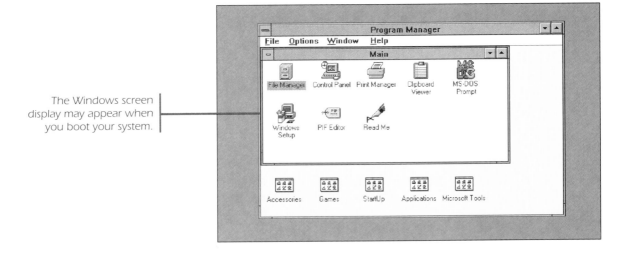

A menu designed specifically for your computer lab may appear. If it does you can usually type a number and press Enter←┘ to load Windows.

The screen may be blank. If it is, turn on the display monitor or adjust its brightness and contrast.

The DOS command prompt may appear. If this happens, type WIN and press Enter←┘.

An error message may read "Non-System disk or disk error." Remove the disk in drive A and follow the instructions on the screen.

COMMON WRONG TURNS: NON-SYSTEM DISK IN DRIVE A

When you boot a system, you may see the error message *Non-System disk or disk error* or a similar message. This appears when you turn on the computer with a disk in drive A that does not contain the operating system files that the computer needs. If you get this message on your system, open the drive door and press any key to continue.

TIP: ARE WE TIMING EGGS HERE, OR WHAT?

When you first load Windows, and at other times when you are using it, you will see an hourglass appear on the screen. This is Windows' way of telling you it's busy and that you should wait before expecting it to do anything else.

TIP: REBOOTING YOUR SYSTEM

Turning a computer on to boot it is called a *cold boot*. Rebooting a computer when it is already on is called a *warm boot*. To warm-boot the system when Windows isn't loaded, you hold down Ctrl and Alt while you press Del. (This command is usually written out as Ctrl + Alt + Del.) Warm booting clears all data from the computer's memory and has almost the same effect as turning the computer off and then back on again. If Windows is loaded, pressing Ctrl + Alt + Del terminates an application program, but you remain in Windows. This is called a *local reboot*. To warm-boot the system, you press Ctrl + Alt + Del again. You normally use this procedure only when you encounter a problem with your system. For example, there are times when Windows "freezes up." You may be able to move the mouse pointer, but you can't execute commands. Whenever possible, you should exit Windows before warm booting your system; otherwise you may lose data.

EXPLORING THE WINDOWS SCREEN

When you load Windows, your screen may look like the illustration shown here. Because Windows can be customized, your screen may look different, but you should still be able to find the elements we are about to discuss.

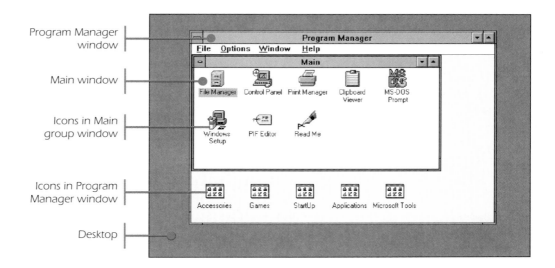

First, notice the boxlike area with a title bar at its top labeled *Program Manager*. This is a *window* about which you'll learn a lot more later. Inside this first window is another window with a title bar labeled *Main*. When working with Windows, it's common to see one window inside another like this.

Inside the Main window are graphical symbols called *icons*. Each icon has a descriptive label, and its design also gives you a visual clue to what it does. In fact, the term *icon* means "a picture, image, or other representation." Well-designed icons accurately represent their assigned function and are easy to remember. For example, the File Manager icon looks like a file cabinet because you use this application to manage the files on your disks.

Below the Main window are a series of small labeled boxes, also called icons. Your screen may display icons in this area that are labeled *Accessories*, *Games*, *StartUp*, and *Applications* and perhaps *Microsoft Tools*.

Notice that the windows and icons are occupying only part of the screen. Around them (and beneath them) is an area called the *desktop*. This desktop is simply the space on the screen available for the display of Windows' various elements. As you'll see, you can add items to this electronic desktop, move items about on it, or take them away from it just as you can on the top of a real desk. In fact, some systems may display one or more icons on the desktop (and not in other windows) when you start Windows. For example, you may see an icon labeled *Vsafe Manager*. This application continually scans the system for signs of viruses that may damage data. If your desktop displays icons, you might ask what they are for.

EXPLORING PROGRAM MANAGER

Windows gets its name because it displays application programs and documents in boxes called windows. All of these windows have many of the same features.

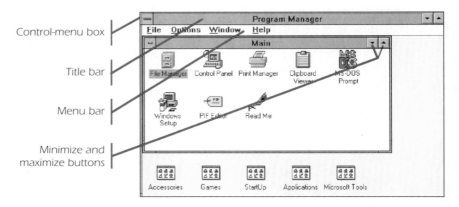

At the top of each window is a *title bar* that lists the name of the application program running in the window or otherwise describes the window's contents.

Every window displays up- and down-pointing arrowheads to the right of the title bar. These are called the *Minimize* (▼) and *Maximize* (▲) *buttons*. As you'll soon see, they are used to change the size of the window.

The upper-left corner of every window displays a *Control-menu box* that displays a Control menu when you click it with the mouse. This Control menu is discussed in the next PicTorial.

A *menu bar* immediately below the title bar displays the names of menus. These menus list commands that you execute to operate your program. Menus will be discussed in detail in the next PicTorial.

EXPLORING YOUR MOUSE

Although Windows can be operated from the keyboard, it is designed to be most effective when used with a pointing device such as a *mouse*. Using a mouse, you can execute commands, specify options, display help, or indicate where you want to type in data. Mice can vary considerably in design, but the most common mouse has two buttons and is connected to the computer by a thin cable.

Turn your mouse over and you may see part of a ball protruding through its bottom (not all mice use balls). When you move the mouse across the table surface, this ball spins and sends electrical signals to the computer through the cable. These signals move the *mouse pointer* on the screen. The mouse pointer is usually an arrow, but it changes shape depending on what it is pointing to and what function it is ready to perform. For example, when it is a single-headed arrow, you can click icons or buttons. When it is a two-headed arrow, you can drag a window's border to make the window wider or deeper.

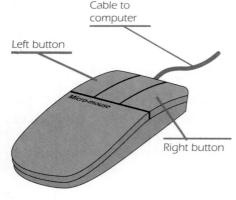

Mouse Pointer Shapes

Normal

Pointing to left or right window border

Pointing to window corner

Pointing to top or bottom window border

Rest your index finger on the left button.

Grip the sides of the mouse with your thumb and ring finger.

PAUSING FOR PRACTICE

Moving the mouse pointer is one of the most fundamental skills you must master. Pause at this point to practice. At first, it seems hard to point to just the right place. Don't be discouraged; it just takes some practice. Pick out an object on the screen, perhaps one of the letters in an icon's title, and then quickly move the mouse pointer to it. Point to window borders and corners until you can accurately make the pointer change shape. Continue practicing until you can move it to any point you want on the first try.

▶▶ TUTORIAL

1. With the mouse cable facing away from you, grip the mouse with your thumb and ring finger.

2. Move the mouse about the desk and watch the mouse pointer move about the screen. This is called *pointing*. If you haven't used a mouse before, you'll see that you need practice to make the mouse pointer move in a predictable fashion. If you run out of room on the desk or mouse pad when moving the mouse, lift it and place it in a new position and then continue moving it.

COMMON WRONG TURNS: MOVING THE MOUSE POINTER

When first using a mouse, most people cannot control the mouse pointer on the screen. It seems to move in unpredictable directions. To gain control, hold the mouse exactly perpendicular to the front of the screen. Now when you move it left or right, the pointer on the screen moves left or right on the screen. When you move the mouse forward or backward, the pointer moves up or down on the screen. If you hold the mouse at an angle other than perpendicular to the front of the screen, it's harder to predict the direction in which the pointer will move.

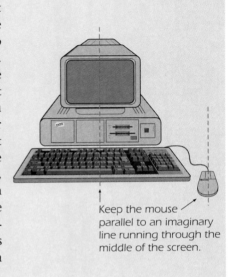

Keep the mouse parallel to an imaginary line running through the middle of the screen.

3. Point to each side of the Program Manager window and you'll see the pointer change shape.

4. Point to each corner of the Program Manager window and you'll see the pointer take other shapes.

CLICKING AND DOUBLE-CLICKING THE MOUSE

Moving the mouse pointer around the screen isn't enough to operate Windows. You must also know how and when to click the mouse buttons. Depending on the situation, you click once or twice.

▶ *Clicking* is quickly pressing and then releasing a mouse button—usually the left one. The finger action is similar to typing a character on the keyboard. (Windows has a command that swaps the functions of the left and right buttons on the mouse. If you are left-handed and having trouble, ask for help.)

▶ *Double-clicking* is quickly pressing a button twice in succession. Double-clicking takes practice.

TIP: USE THE LEFT BUTTON

Since the left mouse button is the one you use most frequently, the terms *click* and *double-click* in this text refer to the left button. If you are ever asked to click or double-click the right button, that button will be specified.

The first question a new user always asks is "When do I click and when do I double-click?" Generally, you click once to select an item and double-click to execute an action. In other words, clicking an item tells Windows you want to use it. Double-clicking starts an application or executes a command.

▶▶ TUTORIAL

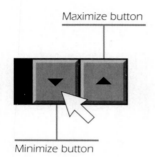

Maximize button

Minimize button

1. With the mouse cable facing away from you, grip the mouse with your thumb and ring finger so that your index finger rests on the left mouse button.

2. Look closely at the title bar labeled *Main* (the smaller of the two windows on the screen), and you'll see two arrowheads, called buttons, to the right of the title. The Minimize button (▼) points down and the Maximize button (▲) points up. Move the mouse until the mouse pointer is pointing to the Main window's Minimize button (▼).

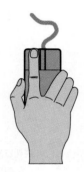

3. Click (the left button) once, and the Main window changes to an icon. It now looks just like the other icons at the bottom of the Program Manager window, but it is labeled *Main* just as the window was.

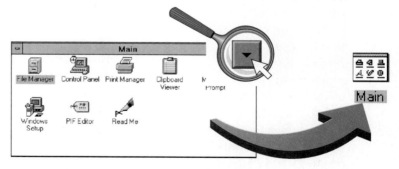

4. Double-click the Main icon to open it up into a window. (If you have problems doing this, see the box "Common Wrong Turns: Double-Clicking.")

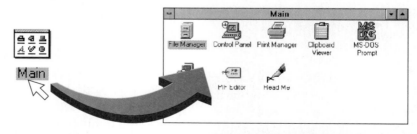

COMMON WRONG TURNS: DOUBLE-CLICKING

The first time any of us uses a mouse, the chances are good that we'll make one of two mistakes. Either we don't click the second click fast enough or we move the mouse with the button held down and this drags something on the screen. To correct these problems, first relax. The mouse moves because you are putting too much force into your action. Just grip the mouse lightly and then lightly click with your index finger. The second click must closely follow the first. If when double-clicking an icon you pause too long between clicks, the Control menu will be displayed above the icon. If this happens, point anywhere but at the icon or menu and click once to close the menu. Just try again until the window opens.

PAUSING FOR PRACTICE

Clicking and double-clicking are fundamental skills for using Windows. Pause here and continue practicing these skills by repeating this Tutorial section until they are second nature. When you are finished, leave the Main group window open.

MINIMIZING, MAXIMIZING, AND RESTORING WINDOWS

A window can be any one of three sizes: maximized so it fills the entire screen or the window that contains it, minimized to an icon, or restored to its original size to occupy only a part of the screen. To change sizes, you use the Maximize, Minimize, and Restore buttons located in the upper-right corner of each window.

▶ Clicking the Minimize button (▼) minimizes the window to an icon. (Double-clicking an icon opens it up into a window of the same size it was before it was minimized.)

Minimize Button
Click to minimize a window to an icon.

▶ Clicking the Maximize button (▲) expands the window to fill the screen or the window that contains it. Once you have clicked the Maximize button, it is replaced by the *Restore button*, which has both an up and a down arrowhead.

Maximize Button
Click to maximize a window to full screen.

Restore Button
Click to restore a window to its original size.

▶ Clicking the Restore button returns the window to its original size.

▶▶ **TUTORIAL**

1. Click Program Manager's Maximize button to enlarge the window to full screen.

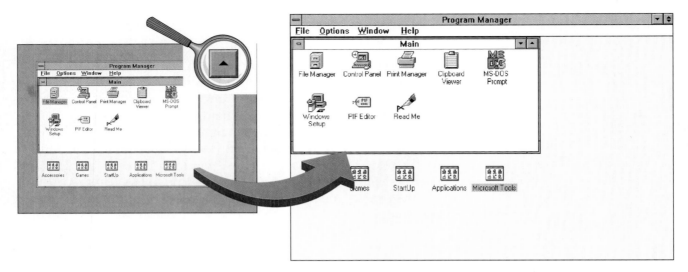

2. Click Program Manager's Restore button to restore the window to its original size.

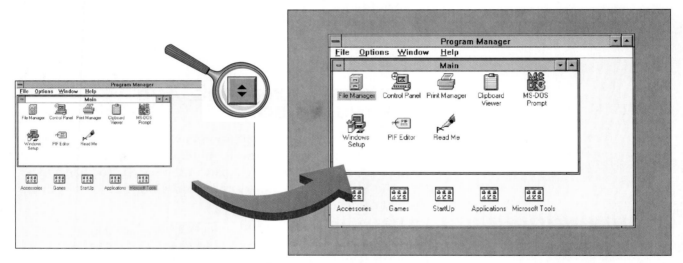

3. Click Program Manager's Minimize button to reduce the window to an icon.

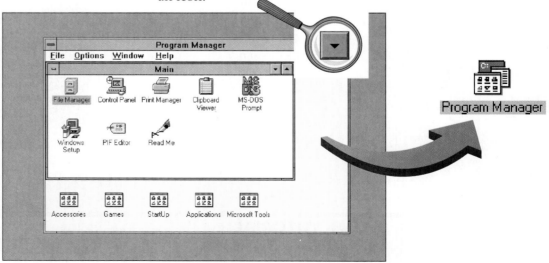

4. Double-click Program Manager's icon to open it back up into a window.

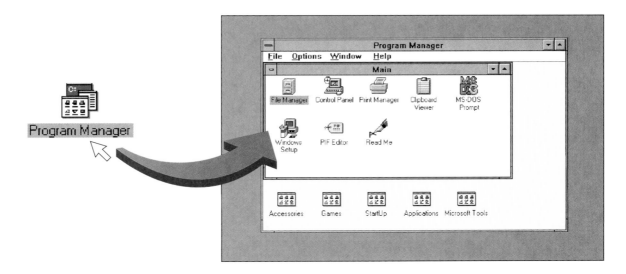

5. Click Program Manager's Maximize button to enlarge the window to full screen.

6. If the Main window is displayed as an icon, double-click the icon to open it back up into a window. Now click the Main window's Maximize button to enlarge it to fill the Program Manager window.

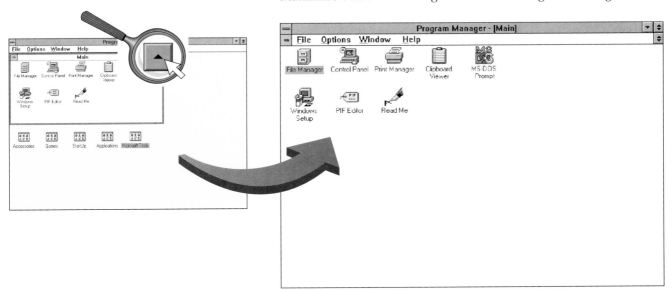

Notice the following about the window:

▶ There appears to be only one window.

▶ There is only one title bar, the one for the Main window, but it contains both names.

▶ There are now two Restore buttons, the upper one for the Program Manager window and the lower one for the Main window.

7. Click the lower Restore button to see what happens.

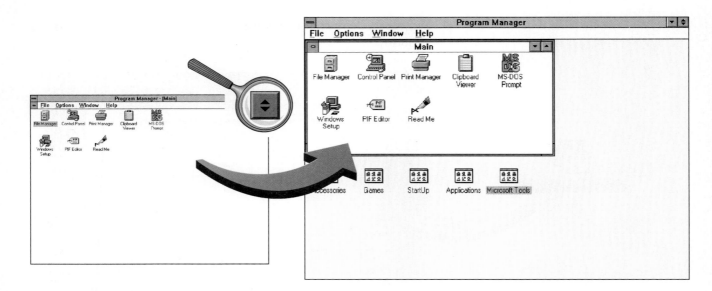

8. Click the remaining Restore button.

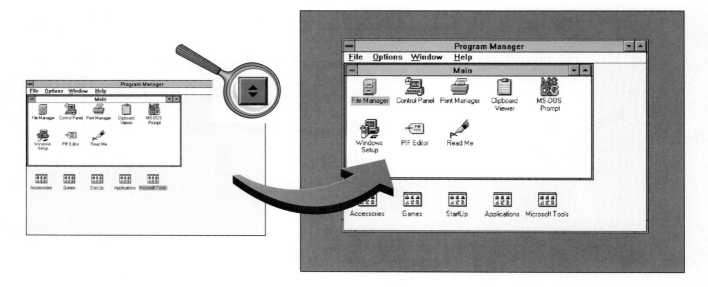

9. Repeat Steps 5 and 6.

10. Repeat Steps 7 and 8 in reverse order to see what happens.

PAUSING FOR PRACTICE

When you work with Windows it's easy to get lost because windows can overlap or hide other windows, making it difficult to find the document or program that you want to work with. You'll only feel at home when you have mastered minimizing, maximizing, and restoring windows. At this point, pause and practice minimizing, maximizing, and restoring the Program Manager window and the Main window until you have mastered the concept and procedures.

EXPLORING PROGRAM MANAGER'S GROUPS

As you work with Windows you will find that there are different kinds of windows and icons. They all work the same, but they are referred to by different names. For example, since Program Manager is an application, its window and icon are referred to as an *application window* and an *application icon*. When Program Manager is displayed as a window, it contains other windows called *group windows* because they contain groups of application icons. When you close one of these group windows to an icon, it is called a *group icon*. Group windows are simply a way to keep related application icons together so the desktop is organized.

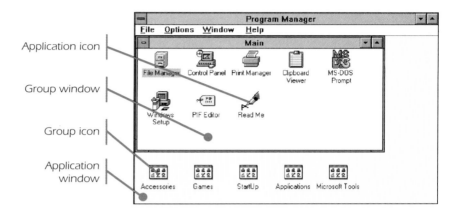

Windows can be easily customized, so group windows and icons vary widely from system to system. However, when Windows is first installed on a computer, its Main, Accessories, and Games group windows are identical on all systems. In addition, there are two group windows that vary widely from system to system. One is the Applications window, which contains icons for the application programs that were on the computer at the time Windows was installed. The other is the StartUp window, which contains icons for the applications you want to run every time Windows is loaded. When Windows is initially installed, the Main group is displayed as a window so you can see its application icons, and other groups are displayed as group icons at the bottom of the Program Manager window.

TIP: DOS 6 AND WINDOWS

Windows runs on top of the DOS operating system, which exists in different versions. DOS 6 is the first version of DOS to be integrated with Windows. It adds a group named Microsoft Tools to Program Manager. This group contains icons that you can use to check for viruses, back up files for security, or undelete files that have been deleted by mistake. You will not see this group window on systems running versions of DOS prior to DOS 6.

▶▶ **TUTORIAL**

1. Click the Main group's Minimize button to reduce it to an icon.

2. Double-click the group icon labeled *Accessories* to open it into a window.

3. Look carefully at each of the icons it contains.

4. Click the Accessories group's Minimize button to reduce it back to an icon.

5. Double-click the group icon labeled *Games* to open it into a window.

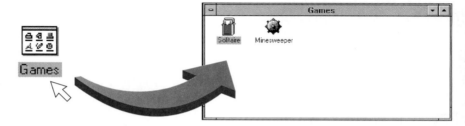

6. Look carefully at each of the icons that it contains.

7. Click the Games group's Minimize button to reduce it back to an icon.

PAUSING FOR PRACTICE

Double-click each of Program Manager's group icons and closely examine the icons it contains. Then click the Minimize button to reduce the window to an icon before opening the next group window. On a separate sheet of paper, write down the names of any icons in the StartUp and Applications groups (and Microsoft Tools if it is on your desktop).

COMMON WRONG TURNS: WHAT TO DO WHEN YOU GET LOST

It's easy to get lost with windows piled on top of windows. If you can't find the data you are looking for, click each window's Minimize button until you find the window you are looking for.

DRAGGING WINDOWS AND ICONS

The desktop can display more than one window at a time. The *active window*, the one you are working in, is always on top of other windows that may overlap it. It may therefore partially or completely hide them. To see one window, you may therefore have to move another. One way to move a window (or an icon) is to drag it with the mouse. *Drag* means to move something on the screen by moving the mouse. To drag an object, you point to it, hold down the left mouse button, and move the mouse to position the object. When you have dragged it to where you want it, you release the mouse button. To cancel a move once you have begun it, you press Esc before releasing the mouse button.

▶▶ TUTORIAL

1. Point to Program Manager's title bar.
2. Hold down the left mouse button.
3. Drag the window to where you want it. As you are dragging the window, its outline is displayed.

Outline of window being dragged

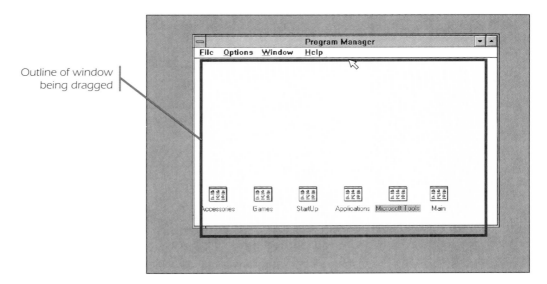

4. Release the left button.
5. If the Main group window is open, click its Minimize button to reduce it to an icon. Now point to the Main icon and hold down the left mouse button.
6. Drag the icon to where you want it and then release the mouse button.
7. Point to the Main icon again, hold down the left mouse button, and drag the icon to a new position but press Esc to cancel the move before you release the mouse button.
8. Click Program Manager's Maximize button to open it to full screen.
9. Double-click both the Main and Accessories icons to open both windows. When you do so, the last one you opened overlaps the first.
10. Point to the title bar of the top window, hold down the left mouse button, and drag the window to a new position. When the windows still overlap but you can see the icons in the bottom window, release the mouse button.

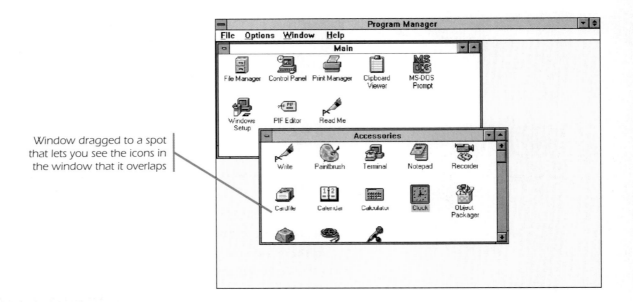

Window dragged to a spot that lets you see the icons in the window that it overlaps

11. Click the visible part of the bottom window to move it to the top and make it the active window. Notice how the title bar of the active window is always highlighted, usually in color on most systems.

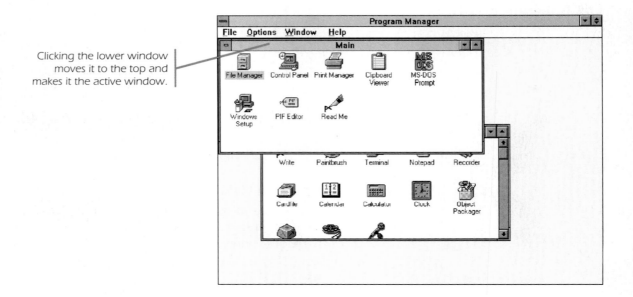

Clicking the lower window moves it to the top and makes it the active window.

PAUSING FOR PRACTICE

Practice dragging windows and icons about the desktop until you feel comfortable with the procedure. Practice pressing Esc in the middle of dragging to cancel the move. With more than one group window open, practice making one after the other the active window.

Dragging the lower (or upper) border makes the window deeper.

Dragging the right (or left) border makes the window wider.

Dragging a corner makes the window both wider and deeper.

CHANGING THE SIZE OF A WINDOW

When you click a window's Restore button, the window returns to its original size. How do you change this original size permanently? You drag one of the window's borders or corners. To do so, point with the mouse to a border or corner so that the mouse pointer turns into a two-headed arrow. Then hold down the left button and drag the border or corner to make the window larger or smaller. When the window is the size you want, release the button.

▶▶ **TUTORIAL**

1. Point to the right side of any open window until the mouse pointer turns into a horizontal double-headed arrow.

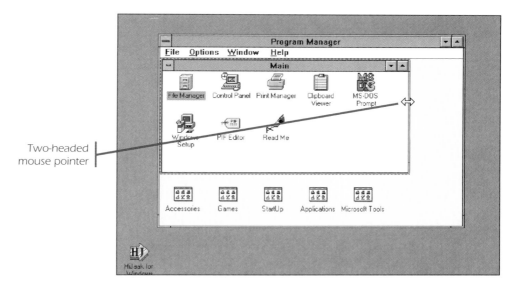

Two-headed mouse pointer

2. Hold down the left mouse button and drag the window wider. As you do so, an outline of the window's new size is displayed.

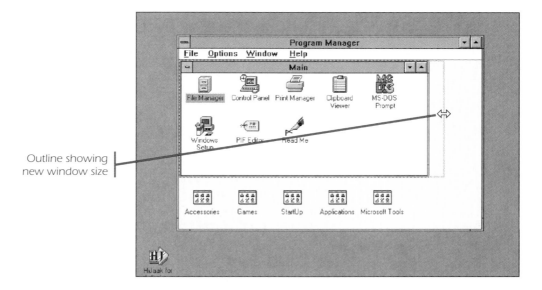

Outline showing new window size

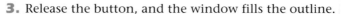

3. Release the button, and the window fills the outline.

4. Point to the bottom of any open window until the mouse pointer turns into a vertical double-headed arrow.

5. Hold down the left mouse button and drag the window deeper and then release the button.

6. Point to the lower-right corner of any open window until the mouse pointer turns into a diagonal double-headed arrow.

7. Hold down the left mouse button and drag the window so it is both narrower and shallower, and then release the button.

PAUSING FOR PRACTICE

Practice changing the size of windows on the screen until you feel comfortable with the procedure. When you make them smaller, some icons may be hidden, but ignore that for now.

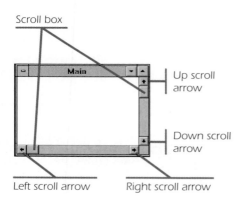

EXPLORING SCROLL BARS

Scroll bars are located on the right and bottom edges of many windows so you can use the mouse to scroll through the contents of the window. Program Manager's group windows display these scroll bars only when they are too small to display all of the icons they contain.

The scroll bar you use to move the contents of a window up and down is called the *vertical scroll bar*. The one you use to move the contents side to side is called the *horizontal scroll bar*. Both scroll bars contains three basic elements: the *up* (or left) *scroll arrow*, the *down* (or right) *scroll arrow*, and the *scroll box*. To scroll the contents of the window a line at a time, click one of the scroll arrows. If you point to one of these arrows and hold down the mouse button, the screen scrolls continuously.

The scroll box, which is sometimes referred to as an elevator because of the way it moves up and down the vertical scroll bar, serves two functions. First, its position on the vertical scroll bar tells you where you are in a window's contents. If it is at the top of the scroll bar, you are at the beginning of the contents. If it is halfway between the top and bottom of the scroll bar, you are in the middle of the contents. If it is at the bottom of the scroll bar, you are at the end of the contents.

Second, the scroll box lets you move quickly to any part of a window's contents. To scroll one screen at a time, point to the scroll bar above or below the scroll box and click. To move to a specific part of a window's contents (such as the middle), drag the box to that part of the vertical scroll bar.

The horizontal scroll bar works the same way. Drag the box to the right side of the horizontal scroll bar to see the right edge of the window's contents.

▶▶ **TUTORIAL**

1. With the Program Manager window open, press [F1] to open the Program Manager Help window. Below the menu bar is a row of *command buttons*.

2. Click the **<u>G</u>lossary** command button to display a list of terms.

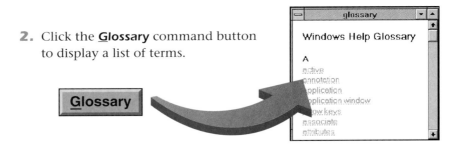

3. Click the Glossary window's Maximize button to enlarge it to full screen. You'll see a vertical scroll bar displayed at the right side of the window.

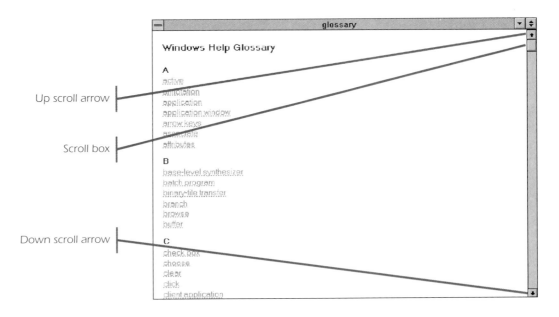

4. Point to the scroll bar's down scroll arrow and hold down the left mouse button until the scroll box reaches the bottom of the scroll bar. This indicates that you are at the end of the document.

5. Point to the up scroll arrow and hold down the left mouse button until the scroll box reaches the top of the scroll bar. This indicates that you are at the beginning of the document.

6. Point to the scroll box, hold down the left mouse button, and drag the scroll box to the bottom of the scroll bar. Then release the mouse button, and you move to the end of the document.

COMMON WRONG TURNS: DRAGGING SCROLL BOX DOESN'T WORK

If you drag the scroll box left or right off the scroll bar when you release the mouse button, the scroll box jumps back to where it was when you started. To be sure the screen scrolls the way you want, release the mouse button only when you can see the outline of the scroll box on the scroll bar.

7. Practice scrolling the window's contents up and down a line at a time by clicking the up and down scroll arrows.

8. Practice clicking the scroll bar above and below the scroll box to scroll a screen at a time.

PAUSING FOR PRACTICE

Practice using the scroll bar until you have mastered the three basic procedures: clicking the arrows and the scroll bar, pointing to the arrows and holding down the left button, and dragging the scroll box.

9. Click the Glossary window's Minimize button to run it as an icon.

10. Click the Program Manager Help window's Minimize button to run it as an icon.

LOOKING AHEAD: RUNNING A PROGRAM AS AN ICON

When you click the Minimize button to reduce an application window to an icon, you do not close the application. It stays open until you issue a command to close it or until you exit Windows.

EXITING WINDOWS

When you have finished for the day, you should always exit Windows to return to the operating system. Windows frequently creates temporary files on the disk. When you exit correctly, these files are closed and all data is stored where it should be.

To exit Windows, click the **File** menu to pull it down, then click the **Exit Windows** command to display a dialog box. Click the **OK** command button to exit or the **Cancel** command button to return to where you were.

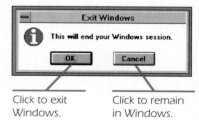

Click to exit Windows.

Click to remain in Windows.

TIP: EXITING WHEN YOU HAVEN'T SAVED YOUR WORK

If you try to exit Windows without first saving your work in an open application, you are prompted to save it and are offered the choices **Yes, No,** and **Cancel**. Click the **Yes** command button to save the file and the **No** command button to abandon it. To cancel the exit command and return to where you were, click the **Cancel** command button.

After exiting Windows, always do the following:

1. Remove any disks from the floppy disk drives. This will prevent their loss, increase security, and ensure that no one mistakenly erases them. (It also prevents the disk drives' read/write heads from leaving indentations in the disks' surfaces.) Make sure you take your own disks with you.

2. Turn off the computer or use the display monitor's controls to dim the screen so that an image will not be "burned" into its phosphor surface or so passers-by cannot see what you are working on. (Windows has a built-in *screen saver* that you can turn on to prevent the screen from being damaged when the computer is left on for long periods of time with Windows running, but it is not available after you have exited Windows.)

TIP: TURNING OFF YOUR COMPUTER

You wouldn't think that leaving a computer on was a major environmental issue, but it is. Computers already account for 5% of all the electricity consumed in the United States, and they are the fastest growing users of electric power. Some 30% to 40% of the U.S.'s 35 million computers are left on overnight and on weekends. New technologies are being developed to lower the power consumption of these idling machines. If their energy consumption is reduced by 40%, it will save carbon dioxide emissions equal to those of 5 million automobiles. Many newer systems are labeled with the Environmental Protection Agency's Energy Star logo. These Energy Star systems, also known as "green machines," consume less power than older models. They also go into a sleep mode when not in use. In this mode, everything remains in memory but power is reduced.

▶▶ **TUTORIAL**

1. Click **File** on Program Manager's menu bar to pull down the menu.

Point to the **File** menu name and click to pull down the menu.

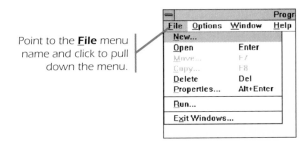

COMMON WRONG TURNS: CLICKING COMMANDS

Many first-time users have trouble choosing commands because they don't point to the right place before clicking. The point of the mouse pointer must be over one of the letters in the command when you click. If it is above or below a letter, even by a little bit, you may execute the wrong command or the menu may disappear.

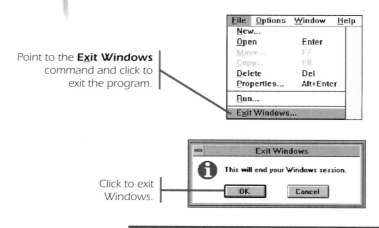

Point to the **Exit Windows** command and click to exit the program.

Click to exit Windows.

2. Click the **Exit Windows** command on the menu.

A dialog box appears telling you that this will end your Windows session.

3. Click the **OK** command button to exit or click the **Cancel** button to return to where you were if you want to continue working.

 ▶▶ **SKILL-BUILDING EXERCISES**

Exercise 1. Loading Windows on Your Own System

List the steps here that you use to load Windows so that you have them for future reference.

1. _____
   _____

2. _____
   _____

3. _____
   _____

4. _____
   _____

5. _____
   _____

NOTE: WINDOWS STUDENT RESOURCE DISK

In Exercise 2, you use the *Windows Student Resource disk*. If your copy of the book does not contain this disk inside the back cover, your instructor will make it available to you.

Exercise 2. Booting Your System

When you turn on your system, watch the lights on the disk drives. You will see the light on drive A flash momentarily as the computer looks to that drive for the files that it needs to start up. If it can't find them there, it looks to drive C. However, if there is a disk in drive A without the needed files, the computer stops and displays the error message *Non-System disk* or *disk error* (or a similar message).

Insert your *Windows Student Resource Disk* into drive A and turn on the computer. You will see the error message that your machine gives in this situation. Write down the error message and the instructions it gives to continue.

_____

_____

_____

Follow the instructions that appear on the screen to continue.

Exercise 3. Using the Windows Tutorial to Learn About Your Mouse

1. Load Windows, point to Program Manager's **Help** menu, and click to pull down the **Help** menu.

2. Point to the **Windows Tutorial** command and click to execute the command.

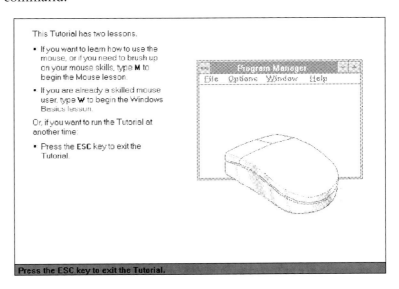

3. Press M to begin the mouse lesson.

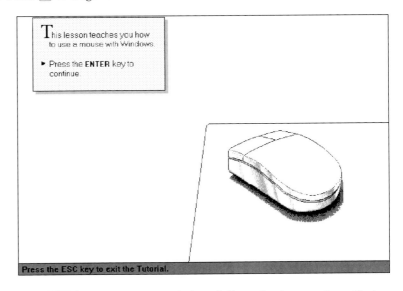

4. Press Enter ↵ to continue, and then follow the instructions that appear on the screen. You can press Esc at any point to end the tutorial.

You use a mouse, like a keyboard, to communicate with the computer.

To use the mouse, you hold it in your hand and move it across a flat surface. If you are left-handed, it might be more comfortable to move the mouse with your left hand.

▶ Type R if you will be holding the mouse in your right hand, or type L if you will be holding the mouse in your left hand

Press the ESC key to exit the Tutorial.

Exercise 4. *Practicing Mouse Skills*

1. Since minimizing, maximizing, and restoring windows is basic to all programs, it is important that you feel comfortable with the procedures. Practice minimizing, maximizing, and restoring Program Manager and its group windows until you feel comfortable. Be sure not to quit until you feel comfortable double-clicking icons to open them.

2. Practice moving and sizing windows by dragging their borders.

3. Maximize all of Program Manager's group icons into windows. Then size and drag them about to lay out the screen as attractively as possible. Drag the icons within the windows into neat arrangements.

PicTorial 1 ▶VISualQuiz

1. For each of these buttons, write down the name and what happens when you click it.

a   b   c

   a. Name: _____   What happens: _____

   b. Name: _____   What happens: _____

   c. Name: _____   What happens: _____

2. For each of these scroll-bar elements, write down the name and what happens when you click (or drag) it.

a   b   c

d   e   f

   a. Name: _____   What happens: _____

   b. Name: _____   What happens: _____

   c. Name: _____   What happens: _____

   d. Name: _____   What happens: _____

   e. Name: _____   What happens: _____

   f. Name: _____   What happens: _____

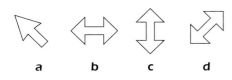

a   b   c   d

Program Manager
a

Accessories
b

3. Describe the circumstances in which the mouse pointer will take each of the shapes shown here.

a. _____

b. _____

c. _____

d. _____

4. Give the specific name for each of these two icons and describe what each reveals when you double-click it.

a. Name: _____ What's revealed: _____

b. Name: _____ What's revealed: _____

5. Name and briefly describe each of the window parts indicated here.

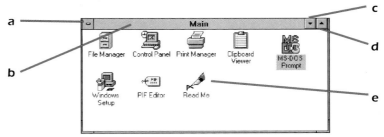

a. _____

b. _____

c. _____

d. _____

e. _____

6. Name and briefly describe each of the scroll-bar elements indicated here.

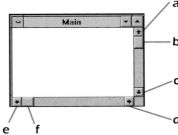

a. _____

b. _____

c. _____

d. _____

e. _____

f. _____

7. Name and briefly describe each of the Program Manager elements indicated here.

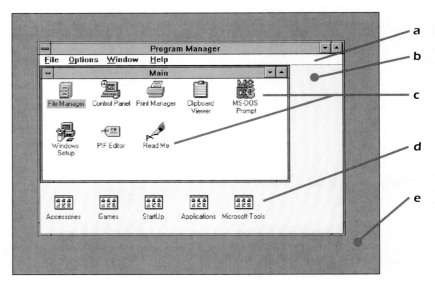

a. _____

b. _____

c. _____

d. _____

e. _____

8. Here is a situation that you frequently encounter when working with Windows.

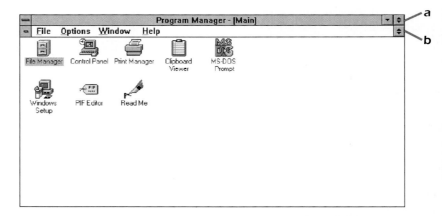

a. Describe what happens when you click the element labeled a.

_____

_____

b. Describe what happens when you click the element labeled b.

_____

_____

_____

9. Name this icon and describe what it reveals when you double-click it.

Name: _____   What's revealed: _____

10. Describe what happens when you click each of these buttons.

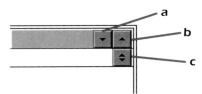

a. _____

b. _____

c. _____

11. How do you display this dialog box? Write down what happens when you click the buttons labeled a and b.

How to display box: _____

a. _____

b. _____

PicTorial 2

Executing Commands and Getting Help

After completing this PicTorial, you will be able to:

▶ Execute commands from menus
▶ Specify choices in dialog boxes
▶ Get on-screen help on commands
▶ Save any changes you make to Windows' screen layout
▶ Practice your skills by displaying the Clock application
▶ Practice your skills by playing Solitaire

Windows makes it easy to issue commands. It's nearly always just a matter of pulling down a menu from the menu bar and then clicking a command on the menu. Either the command is executed immediately or a dialog box appears asking you to specify options or supply more information. On-screen help is available at any point in most procedures.

USING MENUS

In Windows, there is almost always a menu bar displayed on the screen at the top of the active application window. This menu bar lists the names of the menus that are currently available to you.

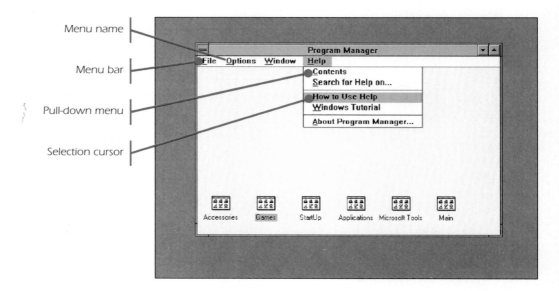

1. To pull down a menu, point to its name with the mouse and click once. (Alternatively, you can hold down [Alt] while you press the underlined letter in the menu's name.)

2. To choose a command from a pulled-down menu, point to the command and click once. (Alternatively, you can press the underlined letter in the command's name.)

If you pull down a menu by mistake, you can click another menu to pull it down or point anywhere outside of the menu or menu bar and click to close the menu without selecting a command.

You can also pull down all the menus in succession and move from one command to another by pointing to a menu, holding down the left mouse button, and dragging the highlight, called the *selection cursor*. Whatever command is highlighted when you release the mouse button is executed. If you decide not to choose a command when dragging the selection cursor like this, point anywhere other than to a menu name or command when you release the mouse button.

▶▶ **TUTORIAL**

1. Click the <u>**Help**</u> menu name on Program Manager's menu bar to pull down the menu. Notice the following about the menu:

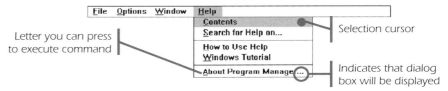

Letter you can press to execute command

Selection cursor

Indicates that dialog box will be displayed

- ▶ The top command is highlighted by the selection cursor.
- ▶ The <u>**A**</u> in the **About Program Manager** command is underlined to indicate you can execute the command by pressing the letter [A]. The ellipsis (...) that follows the command indicates that choosing the command displays a dialog box.

2. Press [↓] and [↑] to move the selection cursor from command to command. Notice how when the selection cursor is on the last choice pressing [↓] moves it to the top. When it is on the first choice, pressing [↑] moves it around to the bottom.

COMMON WRONG TURNS: PRESSING [↓] AND [↑] ENTERS NUMBERS

If pressing the arrow keys enters numbers instead of moving the selection cursor, either press [NumLock] to turn off the numeric keypad or use the other set of arrow keys on the keyboard.

3. Click the **About Program Manager** command to choose it. This displays a dialog box telling you the version of Windows that you are using, to whom the copy of the software is registered, and how much memory is available for your system.

Command button

Registration information

Memory available

4. Notice the **OK** button in the upper-right corner of the dialog box. This is called a *command button*. Point to it and click to close the window.

5. Point to **File** on the menu bar and hold down the left button until told to release it. Notice how some menu commands are followed by a key combination. The listed keys can be used instead of the menu as a shortcut to executing the command that they follow. For this reason they are called *shortcut keys*. You will find shortcut keys listed on many Windows menus.

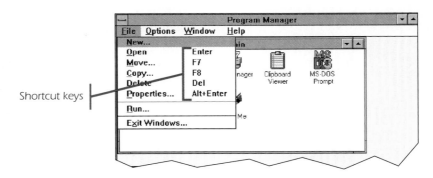

Shortcut keys

6. Without releasing the button, drag the selection cursor first to the right along the menu bar and then back to the left, pulling down one menu after the other.

7. Still without releasing the button, pull down the **Help** menu and then drag the selection cursor down the menu to highlight the **About Program Manager** command.

8. Release the button to execute the command and again display the About Program Manager dialog box.

9. Click the **OK** command button to close the About Program Manager dialog box.

10. Pull down the **Help** menu. (From here on this is how we tell you what menu to use. You now know that to pull it down, you just click its name on the menu bar.)

11. Point to any place but the menu or menu bar and click again to close the menu without selecting a command.

PAUSING FOR PRACTICE

Pause here to practice pulling down menus and then closing them without selecting a command.

USING CONTROL MENUS

Every window has a Control menu you can use to perform some of the procedures you have already learned to perform in other ways. For example, you can click commands on the Control menu to minimize, maximize, or restore windows. You can also click commands that allow you to move or size windows using the keyboard (although these procedures are not covered in this text). The way you display the Control menu depends on whether the window is open or closed to an icon.

▶ If the window is open, there is a *Control-menu box* in the upper-left corner. To display the Control menu you click this box once.

▶ If an application has been minimized so it is displayed as an icon, you display the Control menu by clicking the icon once.

Double-clicking the Control-menu box also provides you with a shortcut to closing an open window. This procedure has different results depending on where you use it. For example, if you double-click Program Manager's Control-menu box, it ends your Windows session. If you double-click an application's Control-menu box, it closes the application. If you double-click a group window's Control-menu box, it minimizes it to an icon.

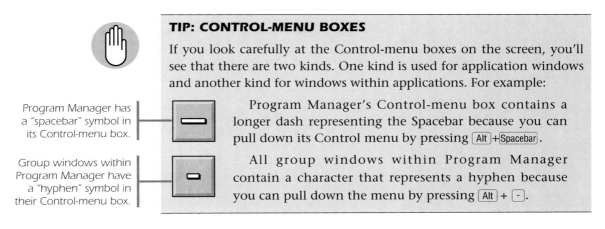

TIP: CONTROL-MENU BOXES

If you look carefully at the Control-menu boxes on the screen, you'll see that there are two kinds. One kind is used for application windows and another kind for windows within applications. For example:

Program Manager has a "spacebar" symbol in its Control-menu box.

Program Manager's Control-menu box contains a longer dash representing the Spacebar because you can pull down its Control menu by pressing Alt + Spacebar.

Group windows within Program Manager have a "hyphen" symbol in their Control-menu box.

All group windows within Program Manager contain a character that represents a hyphen because you can pull down the menu by pressing Alt + - .

▶▶ **TUTORIAL**

1. Click Program Manager's Control-menu box located in the upper-left corner of its window to pull down the Control menu.

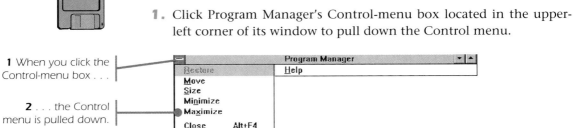

1 When you click the Control-menu box . . .

2 . . . the Control menu is pulled down.

2. Click the **Minimize** command on the Control menu to reduce Program Manager to an icon.

3. Click Program Manager's icon to display its Control menu.

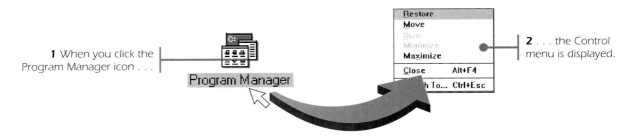

1 When you click the Program Manager icon . . .

2 . . . the Control menu is displayed.

4. Click the Control menu's **Maximize** command to open Program Manager up into a full-screen window.

Pull down the Control menu and click the Maximize command to display Program Manager full screen.

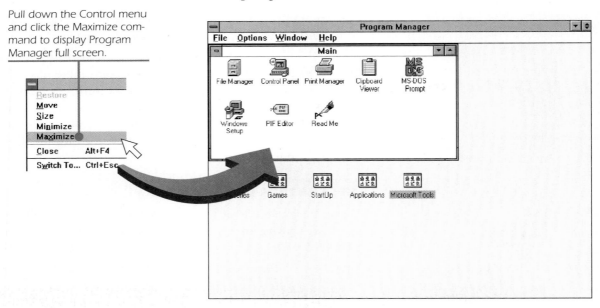

5. Click Program Manager's Control-menu box again to display the Control menu.

6. Click the **Restore** command to restore Program Manager to its original size.

Pull down the Control menu and click the Restore command to restore Program Manager to its original size.

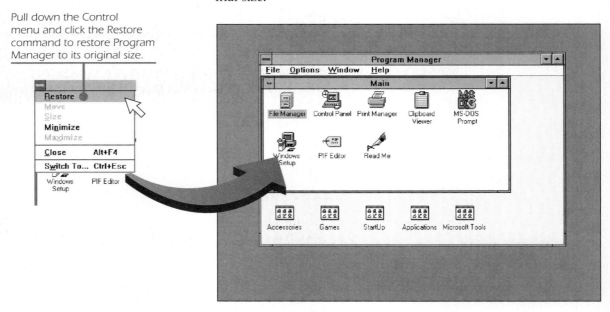

7. Pull down the **Help** menu and click the **About Program Manager** command to display the dialog box.

8. Double-click About Program Manager's Control-menu box to close the dialog box.

Double-click the
Control-menu box
to close the window.

9. If the Main group window is open, double-click its Control-menu box to display the group as an icon.

10. Double-click Program Manager's Control-menu box to display a dialog box warning you that this will end your Windows session.

Click to remain
in Windows.

11. Click the **Cancel** command button to cancel the command. If you had clicked the **OK** command button, you would have exited the Windows program.

PAUSING FOR PRACTICE

Using menus is one of the basic skills you must master. Pause here in the PicTorial to continue practicing using the Control menu to minimize, maximize, and restore both the Program Manager window and one of the group windows such as the Main group. Then practice opening the About Program Manager dialog box listed on the **Help** menu and double-clicking the Control-menu box to close the dialog box.

USING ON-LINE HELP

Windows has extensive *on-line help* available from almost anywhere in any application (only the Clock application has no on-line help). To display help, click the **Help** menu name on the menu bar, click a **Help** command button in a dialog box, or press [F1] at any time. Once you are in the help system, you can choose topics by clicking items on lists, clicking on command buttons, or making choices from menus.

Lists available Help topics

Displays a dialog box so you can search for a specific Help topic

Explains how to use Help

Runs a tutorial on using Windows

Displays version, registration, and memory information

If you press [F1] or click a **Help** command button, the help displayed depends on where you are in a procedure. Since help is *context sensitive*, the help screen describes the procedure you are using and the options you can choose from.

▶▶ TUTORIAL

1. Pull down the **Help** menu and click the **How to Use Help** command to display a list of topics.

Menu names

Command buttons

Terms with glossary definitions are underscored with dotted lines.

Help topics are underlined.

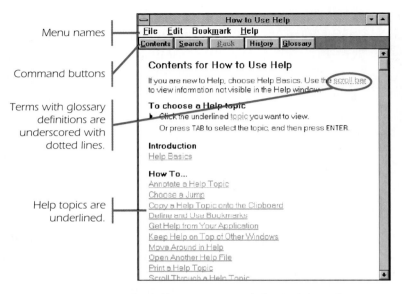

Notice the following parts of the Help window:

▶ A menu bar lists the names of pull-down menus.

▶ Command buttons quickly move you around the help system. Any command button with a dimmed name, such as "**Back**," cannot be executed from where you are in the system.

▶ *Jumps* are underlined words or phrases that jump you to other topics when you click them. Words or phrases underlined with dotted lines display definitions, and those underscored with solid lines jump you to related topics.

2. Hold down Ctrl and press Tab to highlight all of the topic's jumps. Release the keys to remove the highlights.

Pressing Ctrl+Tab highlights all jumps.

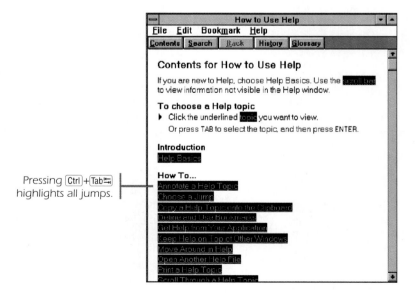

3. Point to the phrase *scroll bar* (a jump) which is underlined with a dotted line, and the mouse pointer turns into a hand with a pointing finger.

When the mouse pointer points to a jump, it takes the shape of a hand with a pointing finger.

4. Click the phrase *scroll bar* to display a definition of the term.

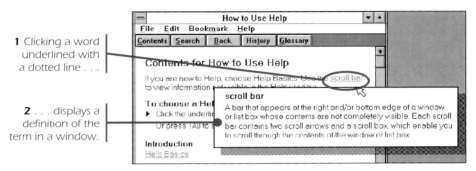

1 Clicking a word underlined with a dotted line . . .

2 . . . displays a definition of the term in a window.

5. Click again to remove the definition. (It's not important where the mouse pointer is when you click.)

6. Click the underlined *Help Basics* to jump to help on that topic.

7. Click the **Back** command button to back up one screen. The **Back** command button becomes dim again because you have backed up as far as you can go.

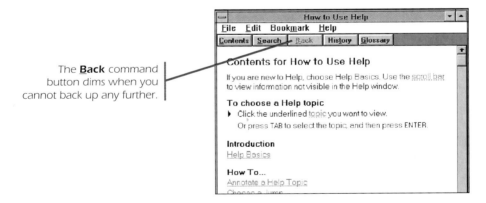

The **Back** command button dims when you cannot back up any further.

8. Click the underlined *Choose a Jump* to jump to help on that topic.

9. Click the **History** command button for a list of the topics you have viewed since loading Windows in the current session. The topic you viewed most recently is at the top of the list.

Clicking the **History** command button displays a list of the Help screens you have viewed.

10. Double-click any of the listed topics to jump to it. This is a great way to return to a topic you viewed earlier.

11. Click the **Back** command button until you return to the screen titled *Contents for How to Use Help*, and the command button becomes dimmed.

12. Click the **Glossary** command button to display a glossary of terms.

Clicking the **Glossary** command button displays a list of terms for which definitions are available.

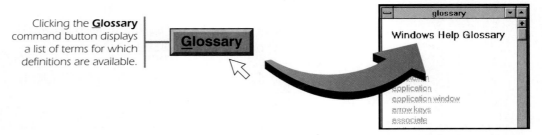

13. Click the Glossary window's Maximize button to enlarge it to full screen.

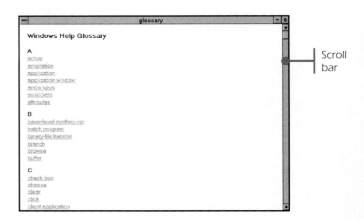

Scroll bar

14. Use the Glossary window's scroll bar to scroll down through the listed terms. You can also press `PgDn` and `PgUp` to scroll through the list.

15. Click any term for a definition; then click again to remove it.

16. Double-click the Glossary window's Control-menu box to close the window and return to Help.

17. Double-click the Help window's Control-menu box to close the Help window.

PAUSING FOR PRACTICE

When working with Windows or any of its application programs, help is always available on line. Knowing how to find the information you need is a very useful skill. Pause here to practice using on-line help. For example, you might look for help on printing help topics and navigating help.

USING DIALOG BOXES

When you choose a menu command, a dialog box may appear letting you supply information about available options. There are many different dialog boxes, but each is made up of elements that include boxes into which you enter text, lists from which you can choose items, and check boxes or buttons that you click to turn options on or off.

TEXT BOXES

Text boxes contain space for typing data. When a text box is empty, you click in it to move to it. An *insertion point* (a flashing vertical bar sometimes called a *cursor*) appears at the left edge of the box. As you type characters, the insertion point moves to indicate where the next character you type will appear.

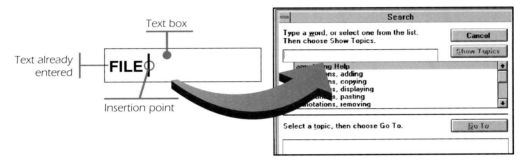

Text box

Text already entered

Insertion point

To edit the text in a text box:

▶ If the text box already has an entry, the entire entry will be selected when you press [Tab⇆] to move to the text box or double-click in it. The first character you type deletes this previous entry. To edit the entry instead, click in the box or press one of the arrow keys or [Home] or [End] to remove the highlight and position the insertion point.

▶ To insert characters, click with the mouse or use [←] or [→] to position the insertion point where you want to insert them, and type them in. The characters to the right move aside to make room for the new characters as you type them in.

▶ To delete a character to the left of the insertion point, press [← Bksp]. To delete a character to the right of the insertion point, press [Del]. Holding down either of these keys deletes characters one after another.

▶ To delete a word and the space that follows it, double-click the word and then press [Del].

▶ To delete adjacent characters or words, move the insertion point to the left of a character, hold down the left mouse button, drag the highlight over adjoining text to select it, and then release the mouse button. (Holding down [⇧ Shift] while you press an arrow key also extends the selection.) When the text is selected, press [Del] to delete it.

LIST BOXES

List boxes display a list from which you can choose an item by clicking it. Lists too long to be displayed in the window can be scrolled with the box's scroll bar.

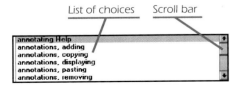

List of choices   Scroll bar

Some list boxes show only a single value and arrows you click to increase or decrease the value.

A *drop-down list box* is displayed as a rectangular box listing only the current selection. To display other choices, click the down scroll arrow to the right of the box.

When you click the up or down arrow, the value increases or decreases.

Here the up arrow was clicked three times.

Drop-down lists have a downward-pointing arrow to their right.

When you click the arrow, a list descends along with a scroll bar.

COMMAND BUTTONS

Command buttons execute commands when you click them. If a button is dimmed, it cannot be chosen from where you are in a procedure.

Commands can also be executed by pressing the underlined button letter on the keyboard.

Dimmed buttons cannot be selected.

A few command buttons contain symbols. If the button's name is followed by an ellipsis (...), clicking it displays another dialog box. If the name is followed by greater-than signs (>>), clicking it expands the current dialog box to reveal more choices.

Clicking a command button with greater-than signs expands the current dialog box.

Clicking a command button with an ellipsis displays another dialog box.

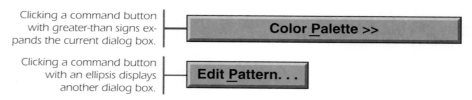

OPTION BUTTONS

Option buttons offer mutually exclusive options (only one can be selected at a time). The one that is on contains a black dot. If you click a button that is off, any other related button that is on automatically turns off.

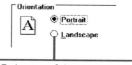

Only one of these option buttons can be on at a time. If you click **Landscape** to turn it on, **Portrait** will automatically turn off.

CHECK BOXES

Check boxes offer nonexclusive options (one or more of them can be on at the same time). To turn an option on, click it to display an X in its box. To turn the option off, click the box to remove the X. If the name of one of the check boxes is dimmed, it can't be chosen from where you are in a procedure.

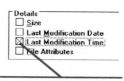

The X in this check box indicates that this option is turned on.

CANCELING COMMANDS

To cancel a command that you have begun but not yet completed, click the **Cancel** command button or double-click the dialog box's Control-menu box.

▶▶ **TUTORIAL**

1. Pull down Program Manager's **Help** menu and click the **Search for Help on** command to display the Search dialog box.

Text box with flashing insertion point

Command buttons

List box with scroll bar

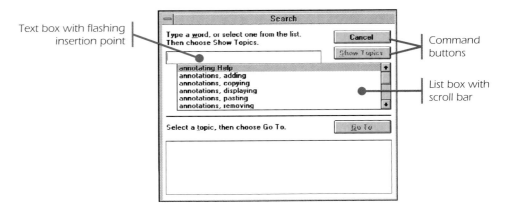

Notice this about the dialog box:

▶ There is a text box with a vertical line, called the insertion point or cursor, flashing in it.

▶ There is a list of topics in a box with a vertical scroll bar. This is called a list box.

▶ There are command buttons you can use to complete or cancel the command.

2. Click *applications, starting* in the list box, and it is automatically entered into the text box.

2 . . . the clicked topic appears in the text box

1 When you click a topic in this window. . .

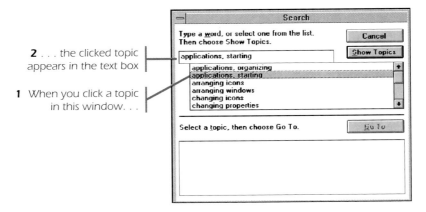

3. Click the **Show Topics** command button to display a list of topics on starting applications in the lower box.

4. Click *Starting an Application from a Group* in the lower box to select it.

5. Click the **Go To** command button to display help on that topic.

6. Double-click the Program Manager Help window's Control-menu box to close the window.

7. Pull down the **H**elp menu and click the **S**earch for Help on command on to display the Search dialog box again.

8. Click *applications, starting* again to enter it into the text box.

9. Point to the text box, and you'll see the mouse pointer change into an I-beam shape.

10. Click anywhere in the box to the right of the word *starting*.

11. Press ⌐← Bksp⌐ repeatedly until you have deleted the word *starting*.

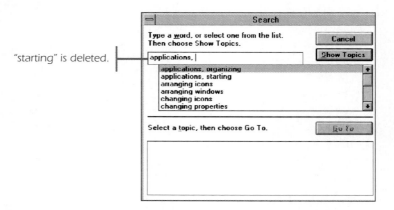

"starting" is deleted.

12. Type **organizing** and click the **S**how Topics command button to list the topics available on organizing your applications.

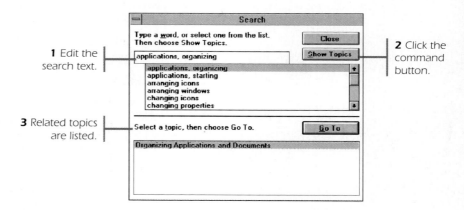

1 Edit the search text.

2 Click the command button.

3 Related topics are listed.

13. Point to the Search window's title bar, hold down the left button, and drag the window to a new position before releasing the button. You'll find that occasionally dialog boxes cover up information you want to see in other windows. When this happens, you can drag them out of the way.

14. Double-click the Search window's Control-menu box to close the window. (Be sure not to click Program Manager's.)

ARRANGING WINDOWS AND ICONS ON THE DESKTOP

When you have a number of windows and icons displayed on the desk-top, they can overlap and hide one another. It may even be hard to find what you are looking for. When this happens, you can use commands on the **Window** menu to jump directly to another window or rearrange items on the desktop. When you rearrange windows, you can have them cascaded or tiled. *Cascaded* windows overlap one another.

Cascaded windows over-lap one another.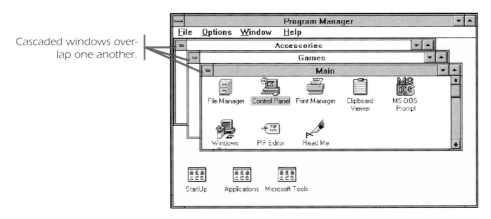

Tiled windows are arranged side by side, much like the tiles on a floor.

Tiled windows are arranged side by side or above one another.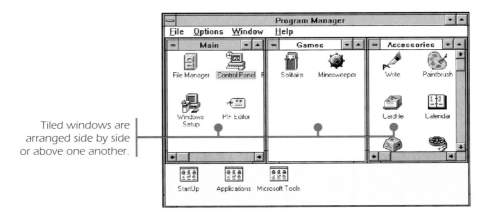

Once you have organized the windows or icons to your liking, you can save the layout. To do so, use one of the following procedures.

▶ Pull down the **Options** menu and click the **Save Settings on Exit** command to remove the check mark (✔) from in front of it. Then press Alt + ⇧ Shift + F4 to save the settings.

▶ Pull down the **Options** menu and click the **Save Settings on Exit** command to place a check mark (✔) in front of it. When you exit Windows, the current settings will be saved. Be sure to remove the check mark the next time you load Windows or subsequent changes will also be saved whether you intended them to be or not.

▶▶ TUTORIAL

1. Maximize the Program Manager window.

2. If the Main, Accessories, and Games windows are not open, double-click each of their icons to open them.

3. Pull down Program Manager's **Window** menu and click the **Tile** command to rearrange group windows side by side. (Your windows may not be in the order shown here.)

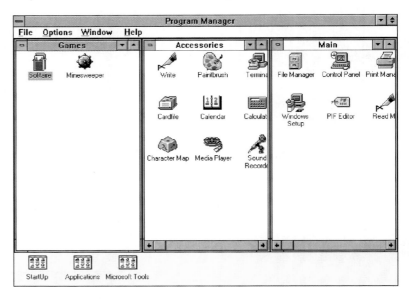

4. Click the Main window to make it the active window. It may have a scroll bar indicating that all of its icons are not displayed.

5. Pull down Program Manager's **Window** menu and click the **Arrange Icons** command to rearrange the icons within the Main window.

6. Pull down Program Manager's **Window** menu and click the **Cascade** command to rearrange group windows so they overlap with their title bars displayed. (Your windows may not be in the order shown here.)

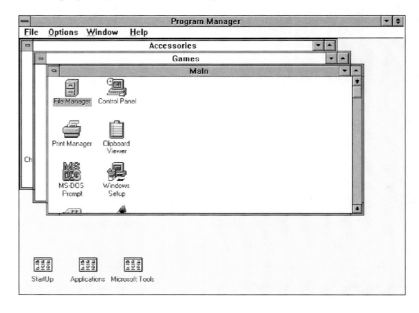

**COMMON WRONG TURNS: WHAT TO DO
WHEN YOU GET LOST**

With windows piled on top of windows, it's easy to get lost. If you can't find the data that you are looking for, pull down the **Window** menu and click the **Tile** command to display all of the open windows at once. If the window you are looking for isn't displayed, it may be an icon that you have to double-click. After locating the window you want, minimize all of the other windows back to icons. You can also press Ctrl+Tab to make one application after another active.

PAUSING FOR PRACTICE

Continue practicing arranging the windows on your desktop. For example, experiment with making different windows active when you execute the **Tile** command. What effect does this have on the position of the active window?

7. Click one of the windows in back to move it to the front of the cascade and make it the active window.

8. Click the Minimize buttons on the Main, Accessories, and Games windows to reduce them all to icons.

9. Drag the icons about on the desk to scatter them in a random arrangement.

10. Click one of the icons to select it and then click the desktop to close its Control menu. The icon's title remains highlighted.

11. Pull down Program Manager's **Window** menu and click the **Arrange Icons** command to space application icons evenly along the lower portion of the Program Manager window.

13. Pull down the **Options** menu. If there is a check mark (✔) in front of the **Save Settings on Exit** command, click the command to remove it. If there isn't a check mark in front of the command, click anywhere but in the menu to cancel the command.

PRACTICING YOUR SKILLS WITH THE CLOCK APPLICATION

One of the application programs in the Accessories group is a clock that can display the time and date based on the computer's built-in clock. If that clock is not set correctly, then the time and date will not be displayed correctly by the clock.

 ▶▶ **TUTORIAL**

1. Open the Accessories group window and double-click the Clock icon to display the Clock on the screen. The time is displayed in analog or digital style.

2. Pull down the **Settings** menu and click the **Digital** or **Analog** command to change the display.

Analog clock display   Digital clock (and date) display

3. If you just set the clock to analog, repeat Step 2 to reset it to digital.

4. With the digital clock displayed, pull down the **Settings** menu and click the **Set Font** command. Write down the name of the font listed in the Font text box.

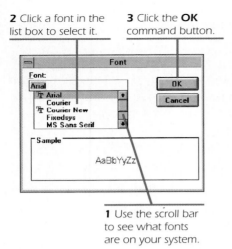

2 Click a font in the list box to select it.

3 Click the **OK** command button.

1 Use the scroll bar to see what fonts are on your system.

5. Scroll the list box to see what fonts are available on your system, click one to select it, and then click the **OK** command button. The Clock is now displayed in the font you selected.

6. Pull down the **Settings** menu and click the **Set Font** command. Change the font back to the original font that was active when you first loaded the Clock.

7. Click the Clock's Maximize button to display it full screen.

8. Click the Clock's Restore command button in the upper-right corner of the screen to display the Clock small.

9. Pull down the **Settings** menu and click the **No Title** command to remove the title bar and menu.

10. Make the Clock as small as possible and drag it around the desktop.

11. Press [Esc] and then click the Maximize button to display the title bar and menu again.

12. Double-click the Clock's Control-menu box to close the application.

TIP: CHEATING?

When you can't find the card you want, hold down [Ctrl]+[Alt]+[⇧ Shift] in Solitaire and when you click the deck, only one card turns over.

BUILDING YOUR SKILLS PLAYING SOLITAIRE

Windows comes with two games, *Solitaire* and *Minesweeper*. Although they are enjoyable to play, the primary purpose for including them here is to let you practice pointing and clicking.

The game of Solitaire is normally played by one person using a deck of cards. Using Windows, you play the game electronically. As you do so, you are able to build your skills in pointing and clicking with the mouse, selecting commands from menus, responding to options presented to you in dialog boxes, and using on-line help.

▶▶ **TUTORIAL**

Opening Solitaire

1. Double-click the Games group icon to display the Solitaire and Minesweeper application icons.

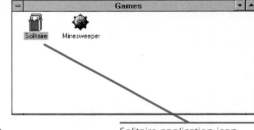

Solitaire application icon

2. Double-click the Solitaire application icon to open up the Solitaire game.

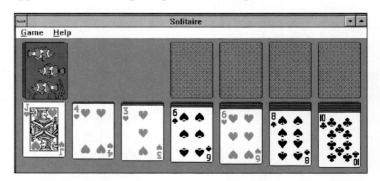

Printing the Rules of the Game

3. To find how to play Solitaire, pull down the **Help** menu and click the **Contents** command.

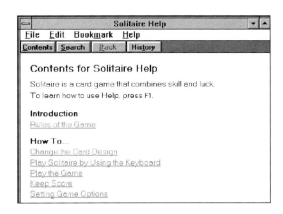

4. Now click the underlined *Rules of the Game* to display a screen listing the rules of Solitaire.

5. Pull down the **File** menu and click the **Print Topic** command to print the rules of the game.

6. Pull down the **File** menu again and click the **Exit** command to exit help.

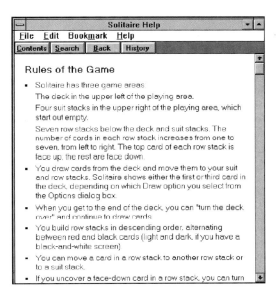

Playing Solitaire

7. To play the game:

▶ Drag any playable card to where it belongs. To do so, point to the card, hold down the left mouse button, and move the mouse. When you have the card positioned where you want it (you don't have to place it perfectly), release the mouse button, and the card jumps to the new position. (Try dragging a card to an illegal position and see what happens when you release the mouse button.)

▶ Turn over additional cards from the deck by clicking the deck once. When all cards have been dealt, click the circle where the deck was, and the deck is ready to deal from again.

▶ To deal a new game, pull down the **Game** menu and click the **Deal** command.

Modifying Solitaire

8. Modify the game following these simple procedures:

▶ To change the design on the back of the cards, pull down the **Game** menu and click the **Deck** command to display various designs. Click the one you want to use to select it, then click the **OK** command button.

PAUSING FOR PRACTICE

Continue playing Solitaire until you are comfortable with all of the procedures you use to play the game well.

▶ To change from turning over three cards at a time to turning over one, pull down the **Game** menu and click the **Options** command to display a dialog box. Click the **Draw One** option button to turn it on. Then click the **OK** command button to return to the game.

Exiting Solitaire

9. Pull down the **Game** menu and click the **Exit** command to close the Solitaire window and display it as an icon.

10. Click the Minimize button to close the Games window and display it as an icon.

▶▶ **SKILL-BUILDING EXERCISES**

1. Exploring Help

1. Pull down Program Manager's **Help** menu and click the **Contents** command to display a list of help topics.

2. Display help on the three menus listed on the screen under the heading *Commands*. After reading each screen, click the **Back** command button to return to the page headed "Contents for Program Manager Help," and then display the next topic.

3. Display help on quitting windows.

4. Close the Help window.

2. Adding Bookmarks to Help Topics

1. Pull down Program Manager's **Help** menu and click the **How to Use Help** command to display a list of help topics.

2. Display help on defining and using bookmarks and take notes or make a printout so you can add bookmarks on your own.

3. Add some bookmarks to various Help screens, move between them, and then delete them.

4. Close the Help window.

3. Annotating Help Topics

1. Pull down Program Manager's **Help** menu and click the **How to Use Help** command to display a list of help topics.

2. Display the various Help screens on annotating a help topic and take notes or make printouts so you can add annotations on your own.

3. Add an annotation to one of the Help screens.

4. Close the Help window.

4. Using the Windows Tutorial to Review What You've Learned

1. Pull down Program Manager's **Help** menu and click the **Windows Tutorial** command.

2. Press W to begin the Windows Basics lesson.

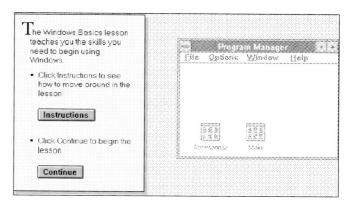

3. Follow the instructions that appear on the screen. Click the **Instructions** command button for advice on how to use the tutorial.

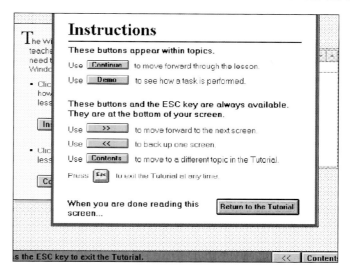

You can press ⎡Esc⎤ at any point to end the tutorial. To resume later, or to jump to another topic, click the **Contents** command at the bottom of the screen. Then click the button in front of the topic you want to learn about.

5. Playing Minesweeper

1. Open the Minesweeper game. (Its icon is in the Games group.)

2. To find how to play Minesweeper, pull down the **Help** menu and click the **Contents** command button. Then click the underlined phrase *What is Minesweeper?* to display a screen listing the rules of the game. Read the information displayed on the screen or make a printout for reference.

3. Play the game following these simple procedures.

   ▶ To mark a square as a mine, point to it and click the **right** mouse button once.

   ▶ To uncover a square that isn't a mine, point to it and click the **left** mouse button once.

   ▶ To mark a square as a question mark, point to it and double-click the **right** mouse button.

- ▶ To change a square marked as a mine into a question mark, point to it and click the **right** mouse button once.
- ▶ To clear a square marked as a mine, point to it and double-click the **right** mouse button.
- ▶ To start a new game, pull down the **Game** menu and click the **New** command.
- ▶ To change the level of the game, pull down the **Game** menu and click the **Beginner, Intermediate,** or **Expert** command.

PICTORIAL 2 ▶VISUALQUIZ

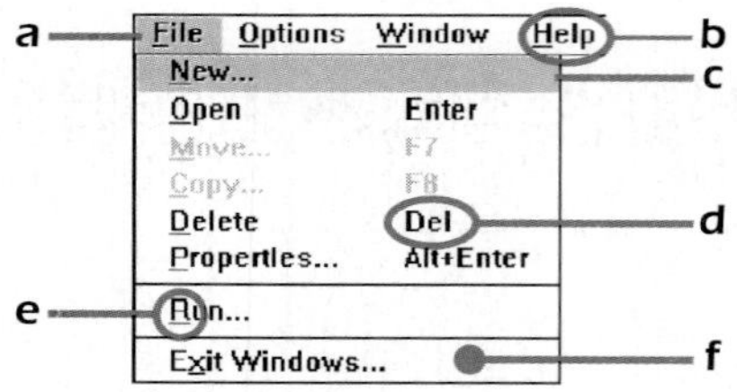

1. The menu shown here has a number of elements or features that you will see on many Windows menus. Write down the name of each of these elements or describe what it is used for.

a. _____

b. _____

c. _____

d. _____

e. _____

f. _____

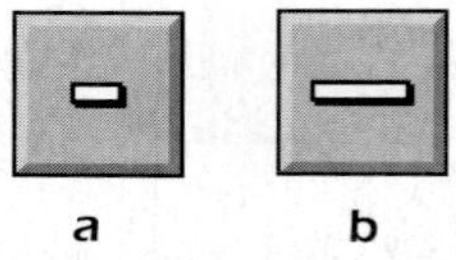

2. Write down the name of each of these elements and what the symbol on each represents.

a. Name: _____ What symbol represents: _____

b. Name: _____ What symbol represents: _____

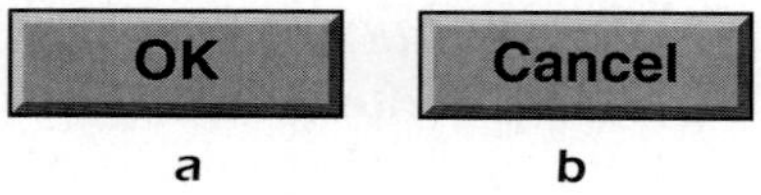

3. Write down the name of each of these elements and describe what happens when you click each.

a. Name: _____ What happens: _____

b. Name: _____ What happens: _____

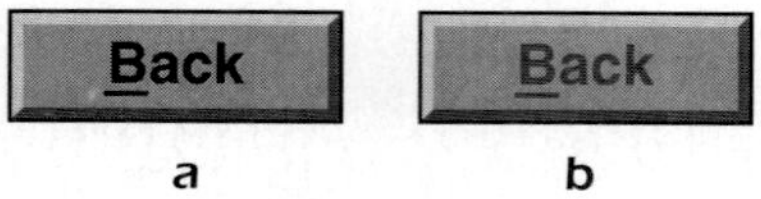

4. Describe the difference between these two buttons.

a. _____

b. _____

5. The ellipsis and greater-than signs on these command buttons indicate something that will happen when you click them. Describe what each symbol indicates.

a. _____

b. _____

6. Give the name of this menu and describe how to display it like this.

_____

_____

_____

7. Describe where you see this icon and what happens when you click it.

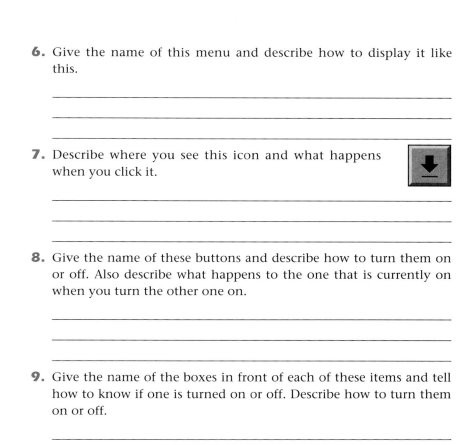

_____

_____

8. Give the name of these buttons and describe how to turn them on or off. Also describe what happens to the one that is currently on when you turn the other one on.

_____

_____

_____

9. Give the name of the boxes in front of each of these items and tell how to know if one is turned on or off. Describe how to turn them on or off.

_____

_____

_____

10. These illustrations show windows arranged in two different ways. Write down the name of each type of arrangement and describe how to arrange windows in these ways.

a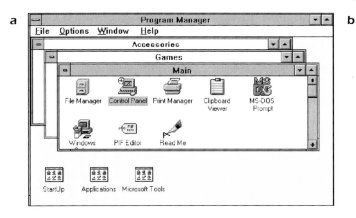

b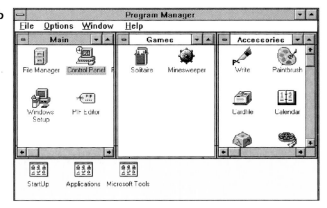

a. Name: _____ How you arrange like this: _____

_____

b. Name: _____ How you arrange like this: _____

_____

11. These illustrations show two types of underscoring that you encounter when using on-line help. Describe what is displayed when you click each.

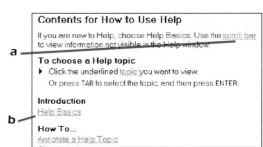

a. _____

b. _____

12. Give the name of each of the items specified in this figure and describe how you use it.

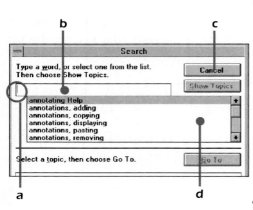

a. Name: _____ How to use: _____

_____

b. Name: _____ How to use: _____

_____

c. Name: _____ How to use: _____

_____

d. Name: _____ How to use: _____

_____

13. Give the name of each of the items specified in this figure and describe each of them.

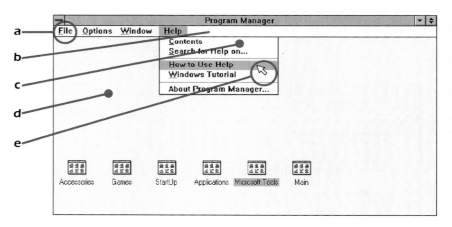

a. Name: _____ Description: _____
b. Name: _____ Description: _____
c. Name: _____ Description: _____
d. Name: _____ Description: _____
e. Name: _____ Description: _____

14. Describe what happens when you click each of the items specified in this figure.

a. _____

b. _____

True-False (Circle T if the statement is true or F if it is false.)

T F **1.** To work on a specific type of application, you use an application program.

T F **2.** To be computer literate, you must be able to design and build a computer.

T F **3.** To boot a computer, you give it a stiff kick in the side.

T F **4.** The drive the computer looks to first when you turn it on is called the startup drive. This drive is always drive A.

T F **5.** When you boot a computer, Windows is always loaded automatically.

T F **6.** Normally, when you boot a computer that has a hard disk drive, there must not be a disk in drive A.

T F **7.** The main function of Program Manager is to make the screen look pretty.

T F **8.** Program Manager is always in memory when Windows is loaded.

T F **9.** The Windows desktop is the screen area where windows and icons can be displayed.

T F **10.** Icons are things that Windows users worship.

T F **11.** Group windows contain one or more application icons.

T F **12.** The Maximize and Minimize buttons display the window at full screen or reduce it to an icon.

T F **13.** The Restore button is displayed only after you have clicked the Minimize button.

T F **14.** Only one window can be active at a time, and it is always the one on top of other windows when they overlap.

T F **15.** To scroll through a document with the scroll bar, you can drag the scroll box to a new position and then release it.

T F **16.** To change the size of a window, you drag the borders.

T F **17.** To drag a window to a new position, you point to the Control-menu box, hold down the left mouse button, and move the mouse.

T F **18.** The mouse pointer is always the same shape, so it is easy to identify.

T F **19.** When you double-click the mouse button, the pause between clicks isn't important.

T F **20.** The only way to pull down a menu from the menu bar is to click it.

T F **21.** To choose a menu command, you double-click it.

T F **22.** The highlight that you can move along the menu bar or up and down menu commands is called the selection cursor.

T F **23.** To close a menu without making a choice, you click it again.

T F **24.** To choose a command button, you just click it.

T F **25.** To display the Control menu, you click the Control-menu box.

T F **26.** To close a window, you double-click the Control-menu box.

T F **27.** The only way to display help is to press ⌨F1⌨.

T F **28.** To display help in the middle of a command, press ⌨F1⌨.

T F **29.** Some words and phrases on Help screens are underlined only to make them stand out.

T F **30.** When the mouse pointer turns into a pointing finger on a Help screen, clicking the mouse takes you to another screen or displays a definition.

T F **31.** To force you to buy books on Windows, Microsoft designed it so you cannot print out help screens.

T F **32.** The flashing vertical line in a text box indicates where the next character that you type will appear.

T F **33.** List boxes list choices you can make by clicking them.

T F **34.** You turn check boxes and option buttons on and off by clicking them.

T F **35.** Only one option button can be on at a time. When you turn one on, the other automatically turns off.

T F **36.** Tiled windows overlap one another on the screen. Cascaded windows don't.

 Multiple Choice (Circle the correct answer.)

1. When you first turn on your computer, it always looks first to ___ for the operating system files that it needs to run.
  a. Drive A
  b. Drive B
  c. Drive C
  d. The drive on the bottom

2. A typical application program is __.
  a. Windows
  b. DOS
  c. Microsoft Word
  d. On-line help

3. If Windows stops working (it "freezes up"), you press __ to perform a local reboot.
  a. [Esc]
  b. [Enter ↵]
  c. [Ctrl] + [Alt] + [Del]
  d. [⇧ Shift] + [Tab ⇆]

4. The sole function of Program Manager is to __.
  a. Provide menus from which you can choose
  b. Launch application programs
  c. Manage the help system for all applications
  d. Manage the memory in your computer

5. The windows containing application icons are called ___.
  a. Application windows
  b. Group windows
  c. Program Manager windows
  d. Document windows

6. When you click a window's Maximize button, the __ appears.

    a. Control menu

    b. Minimize button

    c. Restore button

    d. Icon

7. To close a window down to an icon, you click the ___.

    a. Menu bar

    b. Minimize button

    c. Restore button

    d. Icon

8. To *drag*, you __.

    a. Double-click an object to select it, then click where you want it moved to

    b. Point to an object, hold down both buttons, and move the mouse

    c. Point to an object, hold down the left button, and move the mouse

    d. Point to an object, hold down the right button, and move the mouse

9. To pull down a menu from the menu bar, you __.

    a. Press [Ctrl] and the underlined letter in the menu's name

    b. Click it with the left mouse button

    c. Double-click it

    d. Press [Tab⇆] to highlight it, and then press [Enter⏎]

10. To obtain context-sensitive help in the middle of a procedure, you can always ___.

    a. Click the **Help** command button

    b. Press [F1]

    c. Click the **Help** menu

    d. Ask your lab instructor

11. Dialog boxes provide __ so you can supply information on a command.

    a. Text boxes, list boxes, option buttons, and check lists

    b. Menus and screens of text describing options

    c. Page numbers in the reference manual

    d. A Maximize and Minimize button

Fill In the Blank (Enter your answer in the space provided.)

1. To work on an application, you use a(n) _____ program.

2. If you understand how to use a computer and application software to do useful work, you can consider yourself _____.

3. Windows has what is known as a graphical _____.

4. Turning on your computer is referred to as _____ it.

5. The drive the computer looks to when you first turn it on is called the _____ .

6. If your system freezes up when using Windows, you press _____+_____+_____ to perform a local reboot.

7. To exit Windows, you pull down the _____ menu and click the _____ command.

8. The sole function of Program Manager is to _____.

9. Clicking the Minimize button makes the window into a(n) _____.

10. To quickly close a window, you can double-click the _____ .

11. The windows that contain application icons are called _____ windows.

12. When you minimize a group window, it is displayed as a(n) _____.

13. To open an application, you _____ the application's icon.

14. When windows overlap, the one on top is the _____.

15. To scroll through a document one screen at a time, you click above or below the _____.

16. To scroll continuously through a document, you point to one of the _____ and hold down the left mouse button.

17. When you point to one of the borders of a window, the mouse pointer changes shape into _____.

18. When you click the mouse button once, it is called clicking; and when you click it twice, it's called _____.

19. You can pull down a menu by holding down _____ when you press the underlined character in its name.

20. The highlight that you can move about the menu bar and menus to highlight commands is called the _____ .

21. To close a menu without making a choice, point _____ and click.

22. If a command button is dimmed, you _____ use it from where you are in the program.

23. If a command button displays an ellipsis, clicking it will display _____.

24. If a command button displays greater-than signs (>>), clicking it will display _____.

25. The Control-menu box is located in the _____ corner of every window.

26. If you click the Control-menu box, you _____.

27. If you double-click the Control-menu box, you _____.

28. There are two different symbols in Control-menu boxes. One is like a hyphen and the other a longer dash. The hyphen represents the _____ and the dash represents the _____ because you can pull down the Control menu by holding down [Alt] while you press these keys.

29. You can display help at any time by pressing _____.

30. If you click a word or phrase on a Help screen that is underlined with a dotted line, you display _____ .

31. If you click a word or phrase on a Help screen that is underlined with a solid line, you display _____ .

32. When the mouse pointer changes to a pointing finger on a Help screen, it indicates that you can _____.

33. To edit the entry in a text box, you move the _____ to indicate where you want to insert or delete characters.

34. When you click an option button that was previously off, any other related option button automatically turns _____.

35. If windows are displayed side by side without overlapping, they are_____. If they overlap one another, they are _____.

36. To save any layout changes you make to the desktop, you can press _____+_____+_____.

Projects

Project 1. Describing the Anatomy of the Windows Opening Display

This illustration shows the Windows display that appears when you first load the program. In the spaces provided, write down the name of each of the lettered elements.

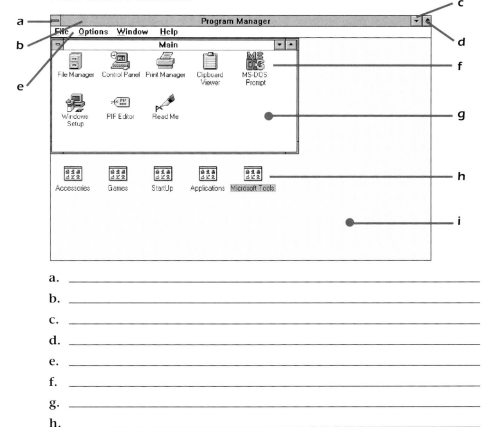

a. _____

b. _____

c. _____

d. _____

e. _____

f. _____

g. _____

h. _____

i. _____

Project 2. Describing the Dynamics of a Windows Display

In this illustration, each of the active elements of the Windows display is lettered. In the spaces provided, indicate whether you click or double-click the element and describe what happens when you do so. (Items a, g, and h actually each have two answers, either of which is correct.)

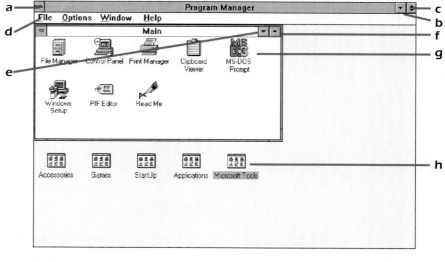

a. ☐ Click ☐ Double-click _____
b. ☐ Click ☐ Double-click _____
c. ☐ Click ☐ Double-click _____
d. ☐ Click ☐ Double-click _____
e. ☐ Click ☐ Double-click _____
f. ☐ Click ☐ Double-click _____
g. ☐ Click ☐ Double-click _____
h. ☐ Click ☐ Double-click _____

Project 3. Describing More Dynamics of a Windows Display

In this illustration, each of the elements of the Windows display that you can drag is lettered. In the spaces provided below, first list the steps you follow to drag an item and then describe what happens when you drag each of the lettered items.

Steps to Drag

1. _____
2. _____
3. _____

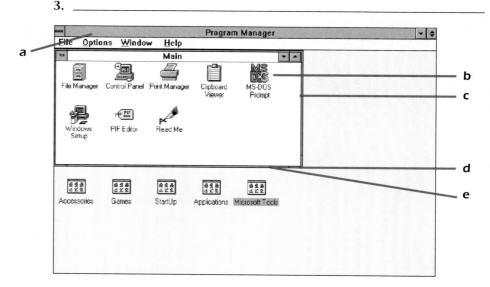

Effects of Dragging Lettered Item

a. _____

b. _____

c. _____

d. _____

e. _____

Project 4. Describing the Dynamics of Help

In this illustration, each of the command buttons on the How to Use Help screen is lettered. In the spaces provided below, describe what happens when you click each of them.

a. _____

b. _____

c. _____

d. _____

e. _____

Project 5. Describing the Dynamics of a Scroll Bar

In this illustration, various parts of a scroll bar are lettered. In the spaces provided below, describe what happens when you click (or drag) each of them.

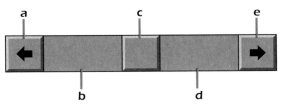

a. _____

b. _____

c. _____

d. _____

e. _____

PICTORIAL 3

FILE MANAGER – AN INTRODUCTION

After completing this topic, you will be able to:

▶ Open and close the File Manager application

▶ Change the selected drive and directory

▶ Describe file icons used to represent types of files

▶ Control the information displayed about files

▶ Display and change a file's attributes

All the data and programs in a computer are stored in files. When you save these files to a disk, you name them so you and the computer can tell one from another. A disk can easily have hundreds or even thousands of files stored in it. To make these files easier to find, you divide the disk into directories so related files can be stored together. File Manager is the Windows application that you use to manage your files and directories.

OPENING AND CLOSING FILE MANAGER

To open the File Manager application, you double-click its icon in Program Manager's Main group. When you do so, File Manager displays a *directory window*.

THE ANATOMY OF THE DIRECTORY WINDOW

The directory window is normally split into two parts. The left half displays a *tree* of the directories on the disk. The right half displays the contents of the selected directory. You can size or move the directory window about the File Manager's workspace or minimize it to an icon.

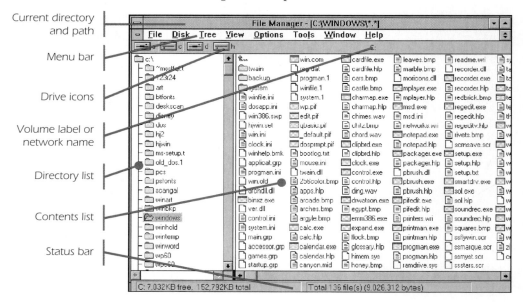

Current directory and path
Menu bar
Drive icons
Volume label or network name
Directory list
Contents list
Status bar

File Manager's directory window has the following elements:

▶ A *directory path* indicates the name of the selected directory (and the path to it, if any).

▶ The *menu bar* lists commands you can use to manage your disks and files. (If your system is using a version of DOS earlier than 6, the menu name **Tools** will not appear on the bar.)

▶ *Drive icons* represent each of the drives on the system.

▶ A *volume label* indicates the name of the disk if one was assigned to it when it was formatted. The name of your network-drive connection (if you have one) is displayed in place of the volume name.

▶ The *directory tree* displays a graphic illustration of how your disk is organized into directories and makes it easy to move between directories or create and delete them. The selected directory is highlighted. The directories are identified by labeled icons that resemble file folders because directories are like folders into which you can place documents to keep your disk well organized. Scroll bars are provided so you can scroll the directory tree if it is longer than the window.

LOOKING AHEAD: DIRECTORIES AND PATHS

Disks can store a lot of files. To keep them organized, you divide the disk into directories that are like file folders in which related documents can be stored. These directories can then be subdivided into subdirectories. Knowing which directory a document is in is important since you may not be able to locate or open a document unless you do. For now, think of a directory as an address. Just as you may live in San Francisco in the state of California, a file may be stored in a directory named DOS on a drive named C.

A path specifies exactly where a directory is on a drive. The elements of the path are separated by backslashes (\), as in *c:\dos*.

▶ The *contents list* displays the files in the selected (highlighted) directory. Scroll bars are used to scroll the contents list.

▶ The *status bar* displays information about the selected drive and selected files. It tells you how many bytes are available on the disk, the number of files in the selected directory and the number of bytes they occupy, and the number and size of selected files (if any). You can turn the display of this bar on and off with the **Status Bar** command on the **Options** menu.

CLOSING FILE MANAGER

When you are finished with File Manager, you can close it. This removes it from the computer's memory and removes its window or icon from the desktop (although the icon remains in the group window). To close, or exit, File Manager, do any of the following:

▶ Pull down the **File** menu and click the **Exit** command.

▶ Click the Control-menu box to display the Control menu, and then click the **Close** command.

▶ Double-click File Manager's Control-menu box.

▶ Press [Alt]+[F4] when File Manager is the active window.

▶▶ TUTORIAL

1. Open the Main group window and double-click the File Manager icon to open the application. (If necessary, click File Manager's Maximize button to enlarge it to full screen.)

File Manager

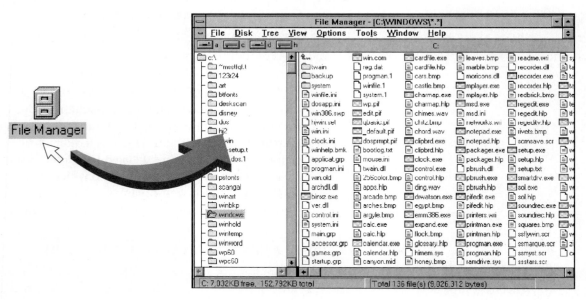

2. Compare your screen with the illustration on page 58 that has parts labeled. (The files and directories listed on your screen will be different from those in the illustration, but the elements of the screen will be the same.) Locate each of the following items on your screen:

▶ Drive icons
▶ The volume label
▶ The contents list

▶ The path to the selected directory
▶ The directory tree
▶ The status bar

3. Double-click File Manager's Control-menu box to close the application. (Click the upper Control-menu box. The lower one is for the directory window.)

4. Double-click the File Manager icon to open the application again.

Double-click here to close File Manager.

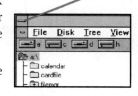

TIP: IF PROGRAM MANAGER REDUCES TO AN ICON

If you find that Program Manager has been reduced to an icon when you exit an application, just double-click the Program Manager icon to open it back up into a window. Then, if you want to stop Program Manager from reducing to an icon, pull down the **Options** menu and click the **Minimize on Use** command to turn it off.

CHANGING THE SELECTED DRIVE

The directory tree and contents list always display the tree and contents of the selected drive, the drive whose icon is outlined by the selection cursor. Different icons are used to represent floppy disk, hard disks, CD-ROM drives, RAM drives, and network drives. One of the drive icons is always selected.

Floppy disk drive icons (also used for other removable media) Local hard disk icon Network drive icon

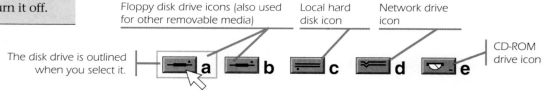

The disk drive is outlined when you select it.

CD-ROM drive icon

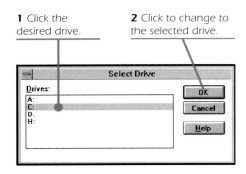

1 Click the desired drive.

2 Click to change to the selected drive.

To change the selected drive, do any of the following:

▸ Click the drive icon.

▸ Hold down [Ctrl] while you press the drive letter. For example, to change to drive C, press [Ctrl]+[C].

▸ Press [Tab⇆] to move the selection cursor to the drive icons, use the arrow keys to highlight the desired drive, and then press [Enter←].

▸ Pull down the **Disk** menu and click the **Select Drive** command to display a dialog box listing all of the drives on your system. (You can also display the dialog box by double-clicking the background area of the bar where the drive icons are displayed.) Select the drive you want to change to, and then click the **OK** command button.

When you change drives, File Manager reads the names of the directories and files on that drive and then displays them in the directory window. If the drive has a lot of directories and files on it, this can take a few moments. (While it is happening, the Windows hourglass is displayed.) You can press [Esc] at any point to stop the process and display a partial tree.

COMMON WRONG TURN: NO DISK IN DRIVE

If you click the icon for a drive that doesn't contain a disk, a dialog box is displayed. Insert a disk and click the **Retry** command button, or click the **Cancel** command button to cancel the command.

TIP: NETWORK DRIVES

You can access any drive on a network if you know its location and password (if any). File Manager displays icons for network drives, and the design of these icons is different from those used to represent other drives. This allows you to distinguish drives shared by other users on the network from those accessible only from your own computer. The procedures you follow to use network drives vary from system to system. However, to begin, pull down the **Disk** menu and click the **Network Connections** command (or a similar command such as **Connect Network Drive**). Enter the drive's path and password in the dialog box that is displayed, and click the **Connect** or **Disconnect** command button.

▸▸ **TUTORIAL**

1. Open the Main group window and double-click the File Manager icon to open the application. (In all of the following tutorials, this step is assumed.)

2. Insert the *Windows Student Resource Disk* into drive A.

NOTE: WINDOWS STUDENT RESOURCE DISK

In this tutorial, you use the *Windows Student Resource Disk*. If your copy of the book does not contain this disk inside the back cover, your instructor will make it available to you.

NOTE: QUITTING

If you have to quit at any point, finish any tutorial you have started, then be sure to remove your disk from drive A. Later you can resume where you left off if you:

1. Double-click the File Manager icon to open it.

2. Insert the *Windows Student Resource Disk* into drive A.

3. Click the drive A icon to make that the selected drive.

3. Click the drive A icon to select drive A. When you do so, the drive's icon is highlighted by the selection cursor. The contents list lists the directories and files on the disk in drive A.

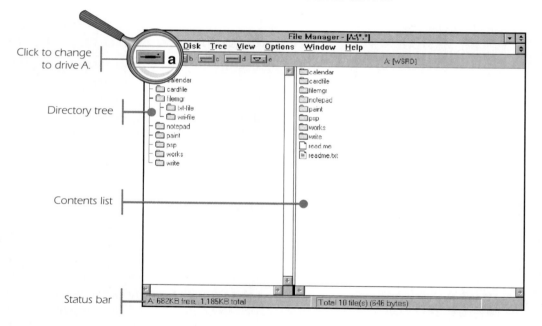

Click to change to drive A.

Directory tree

Contents list

Status bar

COMMON WRONG TURN: OPENING A NEW DIRECTORY WINDOW

If you double-click a drive icon instead of clicking it, File Manager opens a new directory window for the drive on top of the old one. The first window is still open, but it is hidden. To see if more than one window is open, pull down the **Window** menu. All open windows are listed at the bottom of the menu. To close any unwanted extra windows, click the **Tile** command to display them all, then double-click each window's Control-menu box until only one window remains open. (You cannot close the last window, since one window must always be open.)

PAUSING FOR PRACTICE

Selecting different drives is one of the Windows skills that you must master. Pause here to practice changing to each of the drives listed for your system and looking carefully at the listings that result.

4. Click the drive C icon to list its files and directories. (Depending on the speed of your computer and the contents of drive C, this may take a few moments. On some systems you may not be able to select drive C, but there may be another drive available for you to look at.)

5. Look at the status bar to see the disk's free space and total capacity.

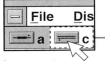

The selected drive is highlighted by the selection cursor.

6. Click the drive A icon to select that drive again.

7. Look at the status bar again to see how much free space is on the disk in drive A and the disk's total capacity.

CHANGING DIRECTORIES

Dividing a disk into directories helps you organize your files better. A disk is like an empty drawer in a new filing cabinet: It provides storage space but no organization. To make it easier to find items in a file drawer, you divide it into categories with hanging folders. You can file documents directly into the hanging folders, or you divide the hanging folders into finer categories with manila folders. A directory is like a hanging folder, and a subdirectory is like a manila folder within a hanging folder. A file in a directory or subdirectory is like a letter, report, or other document within either a hanging folder or a manila folder.

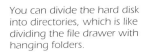

A new hard disk is like an empty file drawer. It has lots of room for files but no organization.

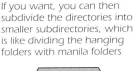

You can divide the hard disk into directories, which is like dividing the file drawer with hanging folders.

If you want, you can then subdivide the directories into smaller subdirectories, which is like dividing the hanging folders with manila folders

You can save files in any of these directories or subdirectories the same way you would file a document in one of the hanging or manila folders.

Directories on a hard disk drive are organized in a hierarchy. The main directory, the one not below any other directory, is the *root directory*. Below it, directories can be created on one or more levels. These directories can hold files or subdirectories. The terms *directory* and *subdirectory* are used somewhat loosely. Strictly speaking, there is only one directory—the root directory—and all others are subdirectories. In most discussions, however, any directory above another is called a directory, and those below it are called its subdirectories.

File Manager's tree lists directories starting at the top of the window with the root directory. All other directories (if any) branch from this topmost directory. When the directory tree is displayed, one and only

TIP: SELECTING DIRECTORIES BEFORE CHANGING DRIVES

When you select a directory on a drive and then select another drive, the directory on the first drive remains selected. When you switch back to that drive, you return to that directory.

one directory may be selected at a time, and it is always indicated by the selection cursor. Most directory and file management commands work only within the selected directory. For example, you can only select a file to be renamed, copied, moved, or deleted from the list of files in the selected directory. If you want to work with a file in another directory, you first have to select the directory in which it is stored. To select a directory, click its name or icon on the directory tree.

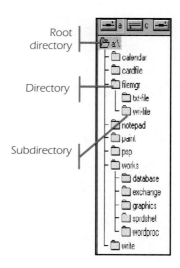

Root directory

Directory

Subdirectory

▶▶ TUTORIAL

1. Insert the *Windows Student Resource* Disk into drive A. If necessary, click the drive A icon to select that drive.

Click to display a directory window for drive A.

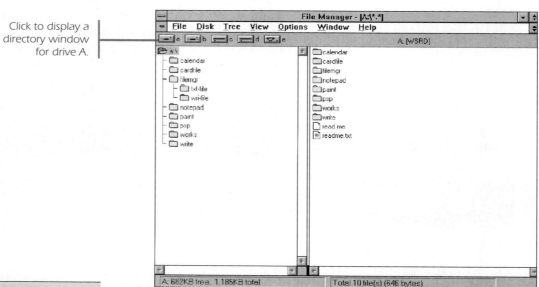

PAUSING FOR PRACTICE

Selecting directories is an essential Windows skill that you must master. Pause here to practice selecting each of the directories listed for the *Windows Student Resource Disk* in drive A.

2. Click each of the directories listed on the directory tree. As you click each directory to select it, notice that:

▶ It is highlighted and its file-folder-shaped icon opens.

▶ The directory's name is listed on the directory window's title bar.

▶ The contents of the directory, if any, are listed in the contents list.

▶ The *filemgr* and *works* directories display file folders on the contents list. These are subdirectories.

▶ The number of files in the directory (counting each subdirectory as 1 file) and their total size are listed on the status bar. (The size of the files in the subdirectories is not included.)

EXPANDING AND COLLAPSING DIRECTORY LEVELS

When you display a directory window, normally only the root directory and first level of directories are displayed; any subdirectories are hidden. You can, however, expand all levels on a entire branch, one more level on a branch, or all levels on all branches in the tree.

To display the subdirectories under a directory, double-click the directory's name or icon on the directory tree. To use menu commands to specify which subdirectories are displayed, pull down the **Tree** menu and choose one of the commands.

Expands selected directory one level

Expands all levels of selected directory

Expands all directories on the tree

Collapses/expands

Marks all expandable directory icons with a plus sign

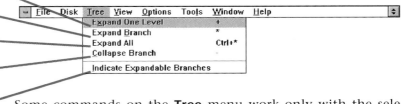

Some commands on the **Tree** menu work only with the selected directory; others work with all directories on the tree. For example, to know which directories on the tree contain subdirectories that haven't been expanded, pull down the **Tree** menu and select the **Indicate Expandable Branches** command. Branches that contain unexpanded subdirectories display a plus sign (+) in their icon. After they have been expanded, this changes to a minus sign (–) indicating that the branch can be collapsed.

Once you have moved down one or more levels in a directory tree, you can also move back up by double-clicking the Up icon—the arrow-shaped icon above the first filename on the contents list.

Up icon at the top of the contents list

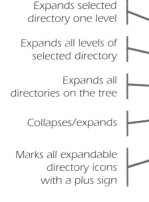

▶▶ TUTORIAL

Getting Ready

1. Insert the *Windows Student Resource Disk* into drive A and select that drive.

Indicating Expandable Branches

2. Pull down the **Tree** menu and click the **Indicate Expandable Branches** command to turn it on. (If it is already checked, click anywhere but in the menu to close the menu.)

▶ Directory icons with a minus sign (–) contain expanded subdirectories.

▶ Directory icons with a plus sign (+) contain unexpanded subdirectories.

▶ Directory icons without a plus or minus sign contain no subdirectories.

Opening and Closing Directories by Clicking

3. Double-click any directory icon marked with a plus sign (+) to expand it. When you do so, its folder-shaped icon opens, its symbol changes to a minus sign, and its subdirectories are displayed.

4. Double-click each of the directory icons marked with a minus sign (–), including the root directory, *a:*. When you do so, its folder-shaped icon closes, its symbol changes to a plus sign, and its subdirectories are hidden.

> **PAUSING FOR PRACTICE**
>
> Double-clicking to open and close directories is a basic skill. Pause here to continue practicing double-clicking directory icons with plus and minus signs until you are sure you understand the principles involved.

Opening and Closing Directories Using the Tree menu

4. Double-click the root directory, *a:*, to select it and display its directories.

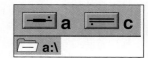

5. Pull down the **Tree** menu and click the **Collapse Branch** command to hide all directories.

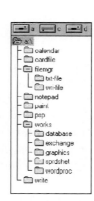

6. Pull down the **Tree** menu and click the **Expand All** command to display all directories and subdirectories on the disk. Notice how there are no directory icons with plus signs because the command expanded all directories.

7. Click the *filemgr* directory icon to select it.

8. Pull down the **Tree** menu and click the **Collapse Branch** command to hide all subdirectories under the selected directory.

9. Pull down the **Tree** menu and click the **Expand Branch** command to display all subdirectories under the selected directory.

Using the Up Icon

10. Click the *txt-file* directory to select it.

11. Double-click the Up icon at the top of the contents list (it is shaped like an arrow), and you move up one level to the *filemgr* directory. That directory is outlined on the directory tree, and its folder icon is open.

Click the Up icon to move up a directory level.

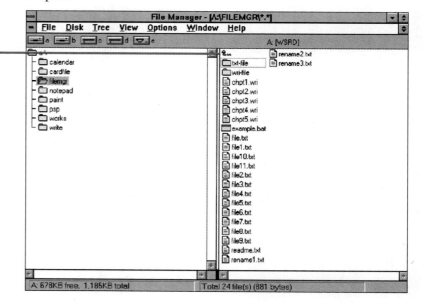

12. Double-click the Up icon again (you may have to scroll it into view), and you move up another level to the root directory. The root directory, *a:*, is now outlined on the directory tree, and its icon folder is open.

PAUSING FOR PRACTICE

Expanding and collapsing the directory tree are basic skills. Pause here to continue practicing expanding and collapsing them by double-clicking and using menu commands until you are sure you understand the principles involved.

EXPLORING THE CONTENTS LIST

The contents list displays the names of files and subdirectories stored in the selected directory so you can locate and manage your files. In order to understand the list, you should know something about Windows filenames. Windows uses the DOS file-naming conventions. You can assign names to files and directories that have up to eight characters and an extension of up to three characters separated from the name by a period.

The file's name can have up to eight characters.

The file's extension must begin with a period and can have up to three characters.

The characters that you can use in a filename are called *legal characters*. Using any other character results in a name the computer will not accept.

Legal Character	Example
Letters	A–Z
Letters	a–z
Numbers	0–9
Underscore	_
Caret	^
Dollar sign	$
Tilde	~
Exclamatioin point	!
Number sign	#
Percent sign	%
Ampersand	&
Hyphen	-
Braces	{ }
Parentheses	( )
At sign	@
Grave accent	`
Apostrophe	'

Filenames that you use should be unique. If you assign a file the same name and extension as a file that is already on the disk in the same directory, the new file can overwrite the previous file and erase it. However, you can use the same name with different extensions—for example, *letter.doc* and *letter.bak*. You can also use the same extension with different names.

Many applications automatically add unique extensions to files that they create. For example, Windows Notepad adds the extension *.txt*, Write adds *.wri*, Paintbrush adds *.bmp*, and the Clipboard Viewer adds *.clp*. Conventions also dictate that some extensions are to be used only in specific situations. For instance, *.exe* and *.com* are normally used for program files, and *.bat* is used for batch files. The extension *.sys* is used for files containing information about your system's hardware, and *.ini* for Windows files describing your system's setup. In many cases, if you don't use the extension the application automatically adds, the application may not be able to identify the file as its own. This can cause problems when you want to open a file later.

Each filename on the contents list is preceded by an icon that indicates its type. For example, program files have a different icon from document files.

| Directories | Program files with extensions .*exe*, .*com*, .*pif*, and .*bat* | Document files associated with an application—double-click to open both the parent application and the document | System or hidden files—be sure not to delete or rename! | All other files |

▶▶ **TUTORIAL**

1. Insert the *Windows Student Resource Disk* into drive A and select that drive.

2. Click the *filemgr* directory to select it and list its files in the contents list on the right side of the screen.

Selected directory

Contents list for selected directory

Status bar information

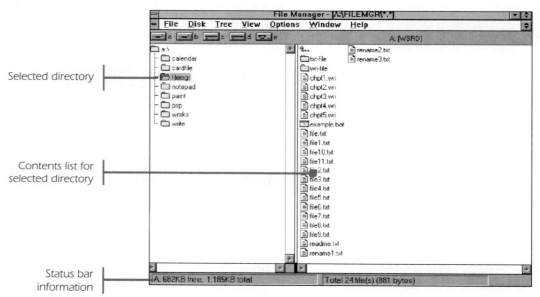

3. Pull down the **View** menu and click the **By File Type** command to display a dialog box.

4. Click all of the check boxes including the **Show Hidden/System Files** check box to turn them all on. (An X in the box indicates that a box is on.)

5. Click the **OK** command button to return to the directory window.

6. Search the icons on the contents list for an example of each of the following types:

- ▶ Directory
- ▶ Document file associated with an application
- ▶ Program file
- ▶ System or hidden file
- ▶ All other files

SPECIFYING FILE INFORMATION
TO BE DISPLAYED

Normally just the names of all files (except those that are hidden) are displayed in the contents list. There are times, however, when it is helpful to display more information about the files. For example, you may want to know their size or the date they were created.

Displays just the names and extensions

Displays file's name, extension, size, date last saved, time last saved, and attributes

Allows you to specify what information is displayed

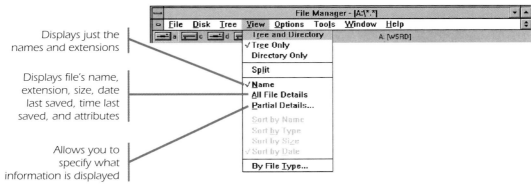

When you first load File Manager, the **Name** command on the **View** menu has a check mark in front of it to indicate it has been chosen and that just filenames will be displayed in the contents list. This is most useful when the active directory has a large number of files since it displays more filenames at one time than any other command.

When you want more information about a file than just its name, you can use the **All File Details** command to display all of the available information about the file.

File size in bytes

Date the file was last saved

Time the file was last saved

File attributes

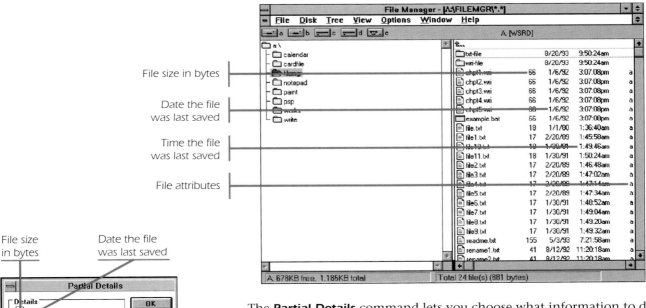

File size in bytes

Date the file was last saved

Time the file was last saved

r (read-only), h (hidden), s (system), or a (archive)

The **Partial Details** command lets you choose what information to display about the files. To display size, date, time, or file attribute information, click the appropriate check boxes to turn them on (X) or off (no X).

When you use the **View** menu's **All File Details** command, the contents list displays the attributes of each file. These attributes are indicated by letters. A file's attributes tell you if the file is a read-only file

(R), a hidden file (H), or a system file (S) and whether the file has been changed since a backup copy was last made with the Windows/DOS Backup command (A for "archive"). You can display a file's attributes, and change them if you like, using the **File** menu's **Properties** command.

▶▶ **TUTORIAL**

1. Insert the *Windows Student Resource Disk* into drive A and select that drive.

2. Click the *filemgr* directory to select it.

3. Pull down the **View** menu and click the **All File Details** command to display filenames, the size of each file, the date and time it was last saved, and its file attributes.

4. Pull down the **View** menu and click the **Partial Details** command to display a dialog box. All of the check boxes have an X because they have been turned on.

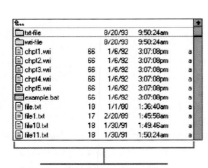

The file's name, size, date, time, and attributes

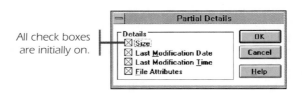

All check boxes are initially on.

5. Click all check boxes with an X other than **Size** to turn them off. Only **Size** should have an X so it's turned on.

6. Click the **OK** command button, and the contents list displays only filenames and sizes.

7. Pull down the **View** menu and click the **Partial Details** command to display a dialog box.

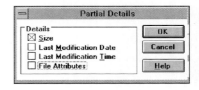

8. Click the **Last Modification Date** check box to turn it on.

9. Click the **OK** command button, and the contents list displays the file's name, size, and last modification date.

10. Pull down the **View** menu and click the **Name** command to display just filenames again.

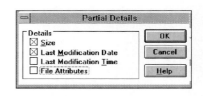

11. Pull down the **View** menu and click the **By File Type** command to display a dialog box.

12. If the **Show Hidden/System Files** command isn't on, turn it on, then click the **OK** command button. Otherwise, click the **Cancel** command button to close the menu without making a choice.

13. Click the *hidden.txt* filename in the contents list to select it.

14. Pull down **File** and click the **Properties** command to display a dialog box listing the file's attributes. Notice that the **Hidden** check box is on.

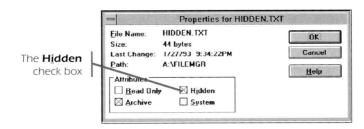

The **Hidden** check box

15. Click the **Hidden** check box to turn it off.

16. Click the **OK** command button to return to the directory window. Notice how the icon for the *hidden.txt* file changes from an exclamation point that indicates it's a hidden or system file to an icon that indicates it is an associated file.

17. Pull down **File** and click the **Properties** command to display the dialog box again.

18. Click the **Hidden** check box to turn it back on, then click the **OK** command button to return to the directory window. The icon for the *hidden.txt* file again has an exclamation point to indicate it's a hidden or system file.

19. To finish the tutorial, pull down the **View** menu and click **By File Type,** then turn off **Show Hidden/System Files** and click the **OK** command button.

SORTING FILES

Normally, files in the contents list are sorted in ascending alphabetical order by name. There are times, however, when it's helpful to sort them in another order. For example, you may want to delete all files ending with the extension *.bak*. Doing so would be easier if the files were arranged by extension so all *.bak* files were together on the list. At other times, you may want to know which are the largest files on the disk. Sorting the list by file size would be helpful in this situation.

Arranges files in ascending alphabetical order (a, b, c) by name

Arranges files in ascending alphabetical order by extension

Arranges files with largest at top and smallest at bottom

Arranges files with most recent at top and oldest at bottom

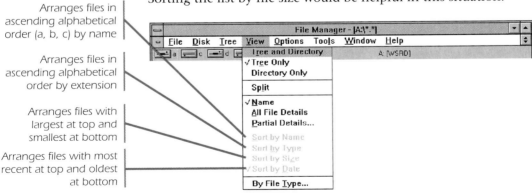

▶▶ **TUTORIAL**

1. Insert the *Windows Student Resource Disk* into drive A and select that drive.

2. Click the *filemgr* directory to select it.

3. Pull down the **View** menu and click the **All File Details** command to turn it on. The files are all listed on the contents list in ascending alphabetical order by name.

4. Pull down the **View** menu and click the **Sort by Type** command to list the files in ascending order by extension. For example, a file with the extension *.bat* is listed before a file with the extension *.wri*. However, directories are always listed first, before filenames.

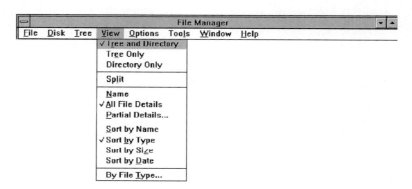

5. Pull down the **View** menu and click the **Sort by Size** command to list files in descending order by file size. Larger files are listed first.

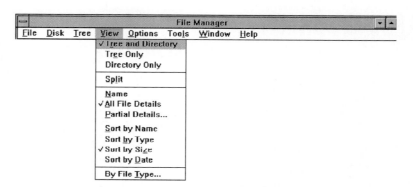

6. Pull down the **View** menu and click the **Sort by Date** command to list files in descending order by date. Those last modified on the same date are subsorted in descending order by time.

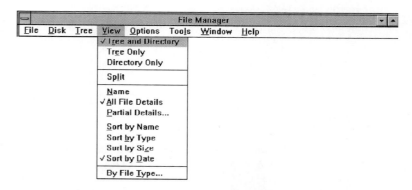

7. Pull down the **View** menu and click the **Sort by Name** command to return the list to its original order.

8. Pull down the **View** menu and click the **Name** command to display just filenames again.

DISPLAYING ONLY SELECTED FILES

When you first open File Manager, the contents list displays the names of all directories and all files in the selected directory (except for system or hidden files). However, you can specify which kinds of files are displayed. To do so, pull down the **View** menu and click the **By File Type** command to display a dialog box. Enter a *filename specification* in the **Name** text box to specify the types of files you want displayed. The phrase *filename specification* refers to any combination of text and wildcards that you enter to control which filenames are displayed. The default filename specification, **.**, displays all files. When you have finished, click the **OK** command button to display filenames based on the choices you have made.

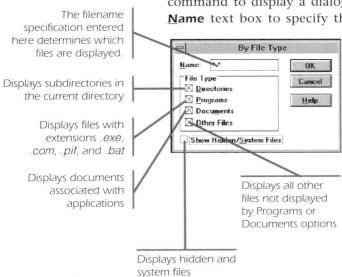

The filename specification entered here determines which files are displayed.

Displays subdirectories in the current directory

Displays files with extensions *.exe*, *.com*, *.pif*, and *.bat*

Displays documents associated with applications

Displays all other files not displayed by Programs or Documents options

Displays hidden and system files

To take advantage of the **Name** text box, you need to understand DOS and Windows conventions for filenames and wildcards. The filename specification you enter into the **Name** text box can contain both text and wildcards. For example, if you want to display only the file named *myfile.txt*, you enter that filename. However, you can also use the ? and * wildcards to specify groups of files. The term *wildcard* comes from card games where a designated card, say a jack, can substitute for any other card in the deck. For example, in the card sequence 4-5-J-7-8, the jack stands for the 6 card.

The wildcard

THE QUESTION MARK

The question mark substitutes for any single character. For example, to display all filenames that begin with *chpt* followed by one or two other characters (such as *chpt1* or *chpt10*) and the extension *.doc*, pull down the **View** menu and click the **By File Type** command, type **chpt??.doc** in the **Name** text box, and click the **OK** command button. The filename specification *chpt??.doc* will display filenames such as *chpt10.doc*, but not *chtp100.doc* because there is no third question mark.

THE ASTERISK

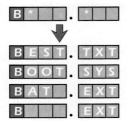

The asterisk represents any character in a given position and all following characters in the part of the filename (either the name or extension) where it is used. For example, to display all filenames that begin with a *c* and have the extension *.doc*, pull down the **View** menu and click the **By File Type** command, type **c*.doc** in the **Name** text box, and click the **OK** command button.

 ▶▶ **TUTORIAL**

Getting Ready

1. Insert the *Windows Student Resource Disk* into drive A and select that drive.

2. Click the *filemgr* directory to select it.

Using the Asterisk Wildcard

3. Pull down the **View** menu and click the **By File Type** command to display a dialog box. The **.** filename specification in the **Name** text box lists all files because the first asterisk is a wildcard that stands for any name and the second asterisk stands for any extension.

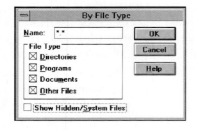

4. Type ***.txt** in the **Name** text box and click the **OK** command button to list all the files with the extension *.txt*. Notice how the filename specification is listed in the directory window's title bar.

5. Pull down the **View** menu and click the **By File Type** command to display the dialog box again.

6. Type ***.wri** in the **Name** text box and click the **OK** command button to list all files with the extension *.wri*.

Using the Question Mark Wildcard

7. Pull down the **View** menu and click the **By File Type** command to display a dialog box.

8. Type **file?.txt** in the **Name** text box and click the **OK** command button to list all files that begin with *file*, have up to one additional character, and have the extension *.txt*. (Note that files with the names *file10.txt* and *file11.txt* are not listed.)

9. Pull down the **View** menu and click the **By File Type** command to display a dialog box.

10. Type **file??.txt** in the **Name** text box and click the **OK** command button to list all files that begin with *file*, have up to two additional characters, and have the extension *.txt*. Now the files with the names *file10.txt* and *file11.txt* are listed.

Finishing Up

11. Pull down the **View** menu and click the **By File Type** command to display a dialog box.

12. Type ***.*** in the **Name** text box and click the **OK** command button to list all files in the directory.

COMMON WRONG TURNS:
ALL FILES NOT LISTED IN CONTENTS LIST

When you enter anything other than *.* when using the **By File Type** command, you should reenter that filename specification before continuing or files you look for later may not be listed. If the **Options** menu's **Save Settings on Exit** command is on, the filename specification you enter is remembered, even when you close File Manager and then reopen it.

CHANGING THE DISPLAY

Commands that control what is displayed

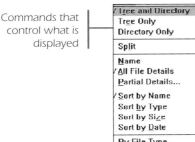

When you first load File Manager, the directory window displays both the directory tree and the contents list. However, you can pull down the **View** menu and choose one of the commands **Tree and Directory**, **Tree Only**, or **Directory Only**. You can switch back and forth between any of these views at any time. When you do so, you display the tree of directories on the disk, the contents of the active directory, or both.

Initially, the directory window allocates the same space for the directory tree and the contents list. If your disk has a lot of levels in its tree or directories have a lot of files, you can drag the *split bar* that divides the windows to make more room in one window or the other. The split bar is located to the right of the scroll bar in the middle of the screen. When you point to the bar, the mouse pointer turns into a double-headed arrow. When this arrow appears, hold down the left mouse button while you drag the bar to where you want it and then release it.

Mouse pointer on the split bar

Split bar

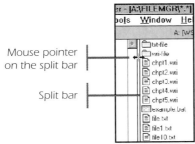

You can also change the font used to display files and directories. To do so, pull down the **Options** menu and click the **Font** command to display a dialog box. Select a font, a font style, and a font size. As you do so, a sample of the font is displayed in the Sample window. When you have selected the font you want to use, click the **OK** command button.

Any changes you make using the **Options** menu are saved automatically when you exit File Manager. However, to save your File Manager screen layout and the settings that you have made on the **View** menu, use one of the following approaches:

▶ Pull down the **Options** menu and click the **Save Settings on Exit** command to place a check mark (✔) in front of the command. When you exit Windows, the current settings will be saved. Be sure to remove the check mark the next time you load Windows or subsequent changes will also be saved whether or not you intended them to be.

▶ Pull down the **Options** menu and click the **Save Settings on Exit** command to remove the check mark (✔) from in front of the command. Then press [Alt] + [⇧ Shift] + [F4] to save the settings.

▶▶ TUTORIAL

Getting Started

1. Insert the *Windows Student Resource Disk* into drive A and select that drive.

2. Click the *filemgr* directory to select it.

Changing the Directory Window Display

3. Pull down the **View** menu and click the **Tree Only** command to display just the directory tree. This tree lists the directories into which the disk has been divided.

Root directory

Other directories

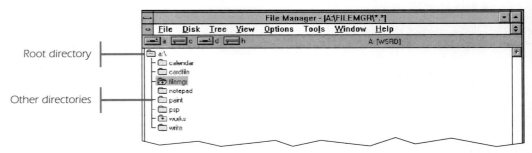

4. Pull down the **View** menu and click the **Directory Only** command to display just the files in the selected directory.

Contents

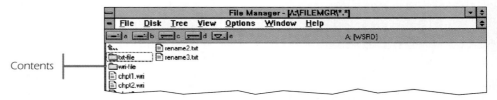

5. Pull down the **View** menu and click the **Tree and Directory** command to display a split screen.

6. Pull down the **Options** menu and change any of the following settings. (A check mark in front of the command indicates that it is on.) You'll have to pull the menu down again for each change:

Turn on

Turn on

Turn off

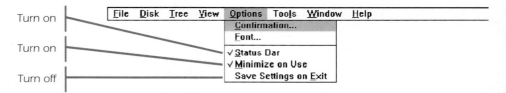

> ▶ Turn off the **Save Settings on Exit** command if it is on. When it is off, any changes you make to the positions of directory windows are not saved.

> ▶ Turn on the **Status Bar** command if it is off. When on, a status bar at the bottom of the screen lists disk and file sizes when you work with files.

> ▶ Turn on the **Minimize on Use** command if it is off. When it is on, File Manager minimizes to an icon when you open another application.

Dividing the Screen Differently

7. Point to the split bar in the middle of the directory window so the mouse pointer takes on the shape of a line with arrows pointing left and right.

Mouse pointer on the split bar

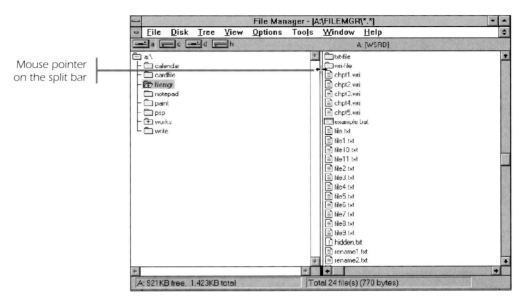

8. Hold down the left button and drag the split bar to the left so there isn't a lot of empty space in the directory tree window.

9. Release the mouse button.

Changing the Font

10. Pull down the **Options** menu and click the **Font** command to display a dialog box listing fonts on your system. The current font, style, and size are highlighted on the three list boxes. Jot down the font's name, style, and size because you'll want to select them again later.

Your font: _____

Your style: _____

Your size: _____

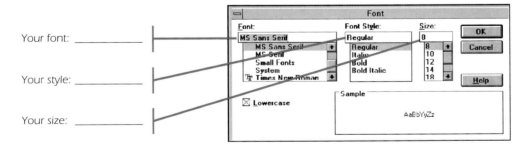

11. Use the scroll arrows to scroll the list of fonts in the **Font** list box and click a different font to select it. When you do so, the Sample box displays the new font.

12. Scroll the **Size** list box and click any font size between *12* and *20* to select it. When you do so, the Sample box displays the new size. (If your system does not list such a size, change the font.)

13. Click the **OK** command button, and the directory window changes to display all text in the new font. What differences do you notice between the original selection and the new one?

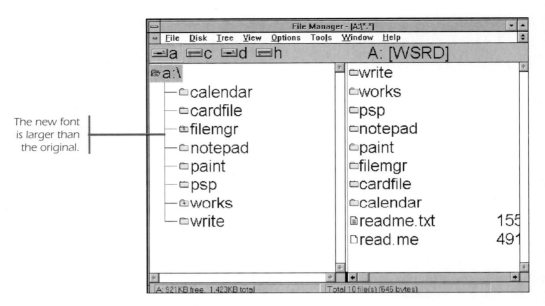

The new font is larger than the original.

14. Repeat Steps 10 through 13 but select the original font and the original size before clicking the **OK** command button.

DISPLAYING, ARRANGING, AND CLOSING MULTIPLE DIRECTORY WINDOWS

To compare the files on different drives or in different directories, you display more than one directory window. This is useful when copying or moving files from one drive or directory to another and especially so when you are dragging and dropping them, as you will see in a later PicTorial.

DISPLAYING MORE THAN ONE DIRECTORY WINDOW

You open another directory window without closing the current one by double-clicking a second drive icon. You can also pull down the **Window** menu and click the **New Window** command to open a window identical to the current one. To display a listing of the files in any directory displayed on the directory tree, hold down ⇧Shift while double-clicking its directory icon. This opens a new directory window, listing just the files in that directory.

When you open a second directory window that shows the same information as the one you opened it from, the windows are numbered. For example, the first may be *C:*.*:1* and the second *C:*.*:2*. Whenever you open one window from another, the new window has the same settings as the one you opened it from. For example, if the directory tree is displayed in the original window, it is displayed in the new one.

Once you have more than one directory window displayed, only one of them can be active. To make a directory window active, do any of the following:

▶ Click anywhere on the window.

▶ Press Ctrl+Tab⇆ or Ctrl+F6 to cycle through the available windows.

▶ Pull down the **Window** menu and choose the window's name from the list displayed at the bottom of the menu to move directly to that window.

ARRANGING DIRECTORY WINDOWS AND DIRECTORY ICONS

To rearrange directory windows, pull down the **Window** menu, then click the **Cascade** command to arrange the windows so they overlap with their title bars displayed or **Tile** to fit all of the directory windows into File Manager's workspace. Normally, tiled windows are displayed one above another. To display the windows side by side, hold down ⇧Shift when you click the **Tile** command. The currently selected window will always be displayed on top or to the left when you tile windows. To change their order, first select the window you want on top or to the left before you click the **Tile** command.

You can also minimize directory windows to icons. To rearrange icons, you can drag them about on File Manager's workspace. To line them up automatically along the lower portion of the File Manager window, select the File Manager window, then pull down the **Window** menu, and click the **Arrange Icons** command.

CLOSING DIRECTORY WINDOWS

One directory window must always be open, but you can close others by selecting them and then double-clicking their Control-menu box.

TIP: QUICKLY CLEARING EXTRA DIRECTORY WINDOWS

Since double-clicking a drive's icon can create a new directory window, you may find many such windows on your screen. To quickly clear them, pull down the **Window** menu and click the **Tile** command. Then double-click the Control-menu boxes on the windows you want to close.

▶▶ TUTORIAL

Getting Ready

1. Insert the Windows Student Resource Disk into drive A and select that drive.
2. Click the root directory, *a:*, to select that directory.

Opening a New Directory Window

3. Double-click the icon for drive C to open a second window for drive C. (You may not be able to tell immediately that it is a second window.)

Moving Between Windows

4. Pull down the **Window** menu; names of the two directory windows should be listed at the bottom of the menu.
5. Click *A:*.* to make it the current window.

Tiling Windows

6. Pull down the **Window** menu and click the **Tile** command to display the two directory windows one above the other. Note that the window for drive A is on top since it was the active window when you executed the **Tile** command.

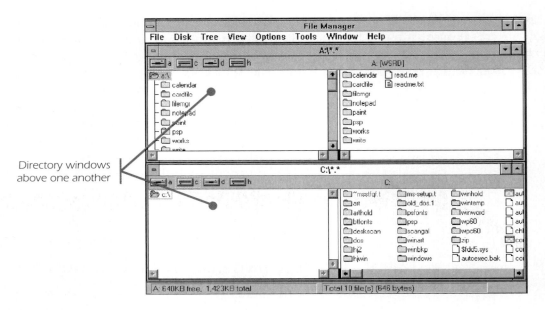

Directory windows above one another

7. Pull down the **Window** menu and hold down ⌂Shift when you click the **Tile** command to display the two directory windows side by side. Note that the window for drive A is on the left since it was the active window when you executed the **Tile** command.

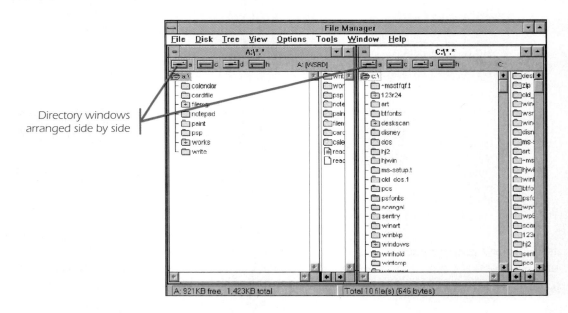

Directory windows arranged side by side

Cascading Windows

8. Pull down the **Window** menu and click the **Cascade** command to display the two directory windows overlapping.

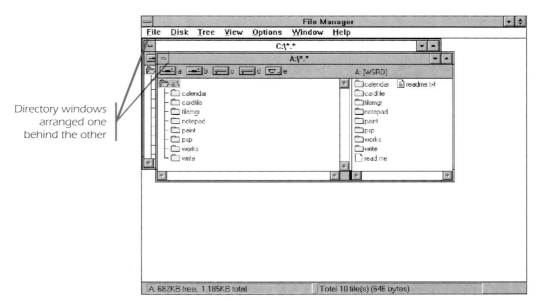

Directory windows arranged one behind the other

9. Click the directory window in the back (the directory window for drive C) to bring it to the front and make it the active window.

Closing a Directory Window

10. Double-click the Control-menu box for drive C's directory window to close the window.

PAUSING FOR PRACTICE

Displaying and arranging directory windows is one of the Windows skills that you must master. Pause here to open directory windows for each of the drives on your system that contains a disk. Practice arranging, moving between, and closing the windows.

▶▶ **SKILL-BUILDING EXERCISES**

1. **Exploring a Useless but Interesting File Manager Feature**

 1. Open the File Manager application.

 2. Pull down the **Help** menu and click the **About File Manager** command.

 3. Hold down Ctrl + ⇧ Shift while double-clicking the Microsoft Windows flag icon in the upper-left corner.

 4. Click the **OK** command button to close the dialog box.

 5. Repeat Steps 2 and 3 to display a dedication with a waving flag.

 6. Click the **OK** command button to close the dialog box.

 7. Repeat Steps 2 and 3 to display a list of credits, presented by a caricature of Bill Gates or one of the other key people behind the development of Windows. The bear stands for the bear that bonks people who introduced bugs into the program during development. If you repeat the series of commands, four different presenters appear in random order.

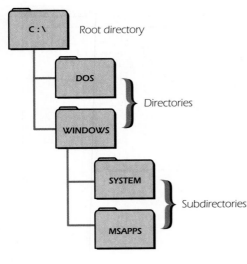

C:\ — Root directory

DOS
WINDOWS
} Directories

SYSTEM
MSAPPS
} Subdirectories

Extension	Number of Files
bat	_____
txt	_____
writ	_____

8. When you get bored, just click the **OK** command button to quit.

2. Exploring the Directory Tree

Use File Manager to explore the directory tree of the hard disk on your system where Windows is stored. You should be able to locate a tree similar to the one shown at the left.

3. Calculating File Sizes

1. Insert your *Windows Student Resource Disk* into drive A.

2. Display the directory window for the *Windows Student Resource Disk*. Can you calculate how much space on the disk is occupied by files?

3. Display the directory window for drive C or any other drive on your system that contains a disk. How much space on the disk is occupied by files?

4. Using Wildcards

1. With your *Windows Student Resource Disk* still in drive A, select that drive.

2. Change to the *filemgr* directory.

3. Using the *.<*ext*> filename specifications, list in the spaces below the number of files there are with each extension. For example, to complete the first entry, use the filename specification ***.bat**. Then list in the table the number of filenames displayed.

4. Be sure to reset the filename specification to *.* when you are finished so all filenames are displayed.

PicTorial 3 ▶ VISUALQUIZ

1. This illustration shows File Manager's directory window. Write down the name of each of the labeled parts in the space provided.

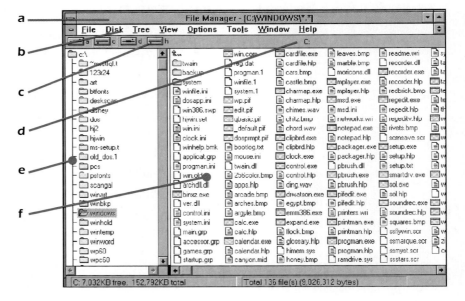

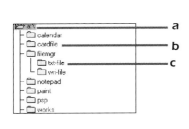

a. _____

b. _____

c. _____

d. _____

e. _____

f. _____

2. This directory tree shows three levels of directories. In the space provided, write down the name of each of the labeled levels.

a. _____

b. _____

c. _____

3. The three folders shown here are from the directory tree. In the space provided, describe what each indicates.

a. _____

b. _____

c. _____

What command do you use to turn these symbols on and off and what menu is it on? _____

4. This illustration shows some typical drive icons. (a) What is the name of the outline around drive A, and (b) what is the major difference between drives A and C?

a. _____

b. _____

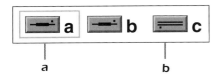

5. What is the name of the element shown here? _____ ⬆️..

What do you use it for? _____

6. Name the two parts of the filename shown here and indicate how many characters can be in each part.

a. _____

b. _____

7. You may see the icons shown here on File Manager's contents list. Describe the type of file that each icon indicates.

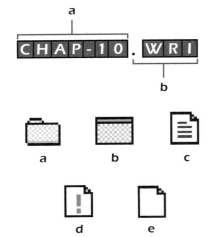

a. _____

b. _____

c. _____

d. _____

e. _____

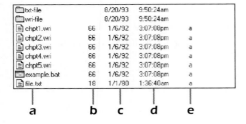

a   **b**   **c**   **d**   **e**

8. There is one major difference between the two contents lists shown here. Explain what the difference is and how you accomplish it.

_____

_____

_____

For the second contents list, explain what information is shown in each of the columns.

a. _____

b. _____

c. _____

d. _____

e. _____

9. Which filenames shown in the left column would be displayed by the filename specifications on the top row? Put a check mark in every box that applies.

Filename	f*.wri	*.*	*.w*
chpt.wri			
file.wri			
file.doc			
new.wrt			

10. Which filenames shown in the left column would be displayed by the filename specifications on the top row? Put a check mark in every box that applies.

Filename	f*.w??	f???.*	n??.w*
chpt.wri			
file.wri			
file.doc			
new.wrt			

11. These two screens show tiled directory windows. Explain how each was tiled.

a. _____

b. _____

a

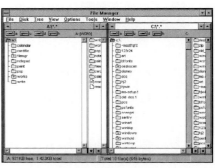

b

PicTorial 4

MANAGING YOUR DISKS AND FILES

After completing this PicTorial, you will be able to:

▶ Format data and system disks and explain the difference between the two

▶ Copy a disk

▶ Label a disk

▶ Organize your files on a disk

▶ Turn confirmation on and off

▶ Search files listed in the contents list

▶ Move and copy files and directories using menu commands

▶ Move and copy files and directories by dragging and dropping

▶ Make directories and subdirectories

▶ Delete and rename files and directories

Some of the operations you perform with File **Manager** affect the entire disk. The commands for these operations are located on the **Disk** menu. They include commands to format, copy, and label disks.

Makes an exact
duplicate of a disk

Adds a label to a disk

Formats a disk

Transfers the DOS system
files to a formatted disk

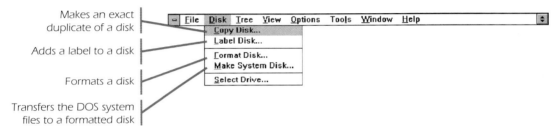

Other operations affect one of more files. For example, you make backup copies of important files in case something goes wrong and delete files when they are no longer needed. At times, you may also want to copy or move files to another disk or change the name of a file or directory. All of these tasks, and many others, can be performed by commands listed on the **File** menu.

Moves selected files

Copies selected files

Deletes selected files

Renames selected files

Changes the
properties of a file

Creates a new directory

Selects files

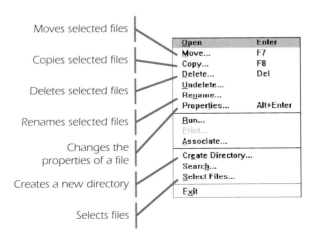

FORMATTING DISKS

A computer cannot store data on a disk until the disk has been formatted for the type of system you are using. Some new disks come already formatted for use with Windows and DOS, but others have to be formatted before you can use them.

Formatting a disk effectively erases any data that may already have been saved on it. You therefore have to be careful with this command. You should never format a previously used disk unless you are sure you will not need any of the files on it. Moreover, you should never format a hard disk drive unless you are willing to lose every file on the disk. (However, since no one is perfect and mistakes do happen, DOS 5 and later versions have an *unformat* command that helps you recover files should you format a disk by mistake.)

Formatting checks the disk surface for unusable spots, divides the disk into tracks and sectors, and creates a directory in which to store a map of the files on the disk. Tracks and sectors are an invisible magnetic pattern on the disk that looks something like the pattern on a dart board. On a formatted disk, tracks run in circles around the disk. Because tracks can store a great deal of data, the computer needs to divide them into sectors, which makes it easier to find a location on the disk. These sectors are like pie-shaped wedges that divide each track into the same number of sectors.

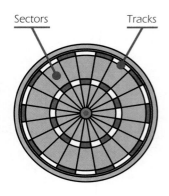

Sectors   Tracks

To store more data, the tracks on some disks are placed closer together. The spacing of these tracks is measured as *tracks per inch* (TPI). The number of TPI determines the density of the disk and the amount of data that can be stored on it. A *high-density disk* (also called a high-capacity or quad-density disk) has more tracks per inch than a *double-density disk* and can therefore store more data—1.2MB as opposed to 360KB for 5¼-inch disks. The maximum density that can be used to store data on a disk is indicated on the disk label and box.

The most common versions of the smaller 3½-inch floppy disks can store 720KB or 1.44MB. These disks can store more data than the larger 5¼-inch disks because they have more tracks per inch than the larger disks. You can tell the two types of 3½-inch disks apart because a 720KB disk has a single square cutout and a 1.44MB disk has two square cutouts.

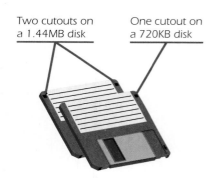

Two cutouts on a 1.44MB disk   One cutout on a 720KB disk

To format a data disk, you pull down the **Disk** menu and click the **Format Disk** command. When you do so, a dialog box is displayed offering a number of options.

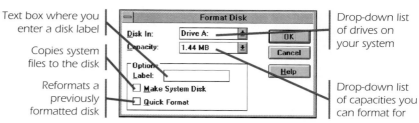

Text box where you enter a disk label

Copies system files to the disk

Reformats a previously formatted disk

Drop-down list of drives on your system

Drop-down list of capacities you can format for

The **Disk In** drop-down list box lists the floppy disk drives on your system. You choose the drive that contains the disk you want to format.

The **Capacity** drop-down list box displays a list of the formats from which you can choose for the selected floppy disk drive. Unless you specify otherwise, Windows formats a disk to match the drive it is being formatted in. However, at times you may want to change the selection to format a 360KB 5¼-inch disk in a 1.2MB drive or a 720KB 3½-inch disk in a 1.44MB drive.

The **Label** text box is where you enter a label for the disk up to 11 characters long. This label is always displayed at the top of File Manager's contents list when you select the drive containing the disk. (You can also add or change a volume label at any time with the **Label Disk** command on the **Disk** menu.)

Turning on the **Make System Disk** check box copies three files needed to make the floppy disk a self-booting system disk for drive A. Disks with these files are called *system disks* because they can be used to boot the system. When you boot the computer with a system disk in that drive, the operating system is loaded from that disk instead of from drive C.

COMMON WRONG TURNS: BOOTING FROM THE DISK IN DRIVE A

Even if a floppy disk is formatted as a system disk, it may not be wise to boot your system from it. The hard disk contains two files that set up your system for you. These are the *autoexec.bat* and *config.sys* files. If you don't copy these two files to the floppy disk, your system will not run the same way when you boot from drive A as when you boot from drive C.

Checking the **Quick Format** check box formats a previously formatted disk. This form of formatting is faster than a normal format because it does not check the disk for bad sectors. When DOS formats a disk, bad or defective sectors are normally marked so data isn't stored on them. Since the quick format doesn't check for them, don't use this command unless you know the disk is in good shape.

▶▶ TUTORIAL

1. Load Windows and double-click the File Manager icon to open it.

2. Label a blank floppy disk for drive A of your computer, using as a guide the label shown here. **Be sure the disk does not contain any data that you want to save because formatting it will erase the data!**

3. Insert your newly labeled disk into drive A.

4. Pull down the **Disk** menu and click the **Format Disk** command to display a dialog box. The command automatically selects drive A to format, but your **Capacity** setting may be different from the one illustrated here, depending on what type of drive A your system has.

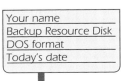

Your name
Backup Resource Disk
DOS format
Today's date

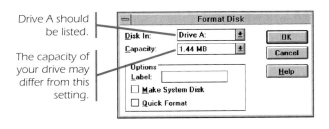

Drive A should be listed.

The capacity of your drive may differ from this setting.

5. Click in the **Label** text box to move the insertion point there, then type your first name (abbreviating it to 11 characters if necessary).

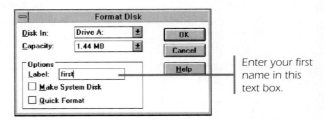

Enter your first name in this text box.

6. Click the **OK** command button to display the Confirm Format Disk dialog box.

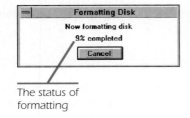

The status of formatting

7. Click the **Yes** command button, and the drive spins and its light comes on as the disk is formatted. A box displays the status of the formatting procedure.

When the disk has been formatted, the Format Complete box appears. This box tells you how much total space is on the disk and how much is available for your files. A prompt asks you if you want to format another disk.

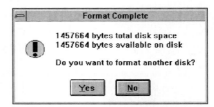

8. Click the **No** command button, and you return to File Manager. Your first name, which you entered as the disk's label, should be displayed at the top of the contents list. If it isn't, pull down the **Window** menu and click the **Refresh** command.

COPYING DISKS

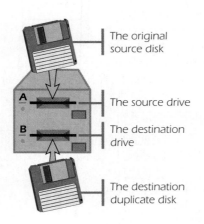

The original source disk

The source drive

The destination drive

The destination duplicate disk

To make an exact copy of a disk, you use the **Copy Disk** command on File Manager's **Disk** menu. When you choose this command, a dialog box appears if your system has more than one floppy disk drive. The dialog box contains two drop-down list boxes you use to specify the source and destination drives. When using this command, keep the following points in mind:

▶ The destination disk will be formatted as part of the process, if necessary, before files are copied to it.

▶ If you use this command to copy files to a disk that already contains files, the existing files will be erased.

▶ You can only use the **Copy Disk** command to copy files between disks with identical storage capacities. For example, you cannot use **Copy Disk** between a high-density 5¼-inch disk and a disk in a 360KB drive. And you cannot use this command between 5¼-inch and 3½-inch drives.

▶ The command copies not only files but also directories and sub-directories.

TIP: WRITE-PROTECTING YOUR DISKS

When you work with files and disks, you can lose work if you make a mistake. To protect important files, write-protect the disk. If a disk is write-protected, you can read files on the disk, but you cannot save files on it, format it, or erase files from it.

Tape

Write-protect notch

Write-protected when window is open

Not write-protected when closed

▶ To write-protect a 5¼-inch floppy disk, cover the write-protect notch with a piece of tape. You must use a write-protect tape that light cannot shine through since some drives use a light to determine whether the notch is covered. If you use a transparent tape, the light will shine through the notch just as if it were not covered, and the drive will assume it is not write-protected.

▶ To write-protect a 3½-inch floppy disk, open the sliding tab in the write-protect window.

Why do you write-protect one type of disk by *covering* the notch and the other by *uncovering* the window? If you are paranoid and believe in conspiracies, this may be evidence you need to prove that there is a plot to make computers as difficult as possible!

▶▶ **TUTORIAL**

1. Insert the **write-protected** original *Windows Student Resource Disk* into drive A and select that drive.

Original

2. Pull down the **Disk** menu and click the **Copy Disk** command. What then happens depends on your system:

▶ If your system has only one floppy disk drive, the Confirm Copy Disk dialog box appears. Proceed to Step 3.

Confirm Copy Disk

This operation will erase ALL data from the destination disk. Are you sure you want to continue?

[Yes]   [No]

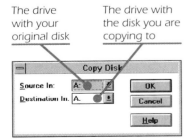

The drive with your original disk

The drive with the disk you are copying to

Copy Disk

Source In: A.
Destination In: A.

[OK]
[Cancel]
[Help]

▶ If your system has two floppy disk drives, a dialog box is displayed with two drop-down list boxes showing the source and destination drives. The source is the drive you are copying from (drive A) and the destination is the drive you are copying the disk to.

▶ If your system has two drives but they don't match, leave both drives set to A. Click the **OK** command button, and the Confirm Copy Disk dialog box appears.

With the original Windows Student Resource Disk in drive A, click to continue.

▶ If your system has more than one drive of the same type, pull down the **Destination In** list box and select the drive you are copying to (usually drive B). Click the **OK** command button, and the Confirm Copy Disk dialog box appears.

3. Click the **Yes** command button, and the dialog box asks you to insert the source disk.

4. You have already done so, so click the **OK** command button to begin copying. A Copying Disk dialog box keeps you posted on the copying progress. If you left both source and destination drives set to drive A, dialog boxes may periodically appear asking you to swap disks:

▶ When the prompt *Insert destination disk* appears, insert the *Backup Resource Disk* you formatted in the preceding tutorial and click the **OK** command button to continue.

▶ When the prompt *Insert source disk* appears, insert the original *Windows Student Resource Disk* and click the **OK** command button to continue. When the dialog box disappears, the disk has been copied and is identical to the original disk. However, note that the disk's label above the contents list still shows your first name as the disk's label. This is because the directory window has not been updated.

5. Pull down the **Window** menu and click the **Refresh** command to update the directory window. The disk's label changes to *[WSRD]*.

6. Save this disk to use throughout the rest of this text. It is your *Backup Resource Disk*. From this point on, you should use this disk when the tutorials specify the *Windows Student Resource Disk*.

TIP: STORE YOUR WINDOWS STUDENT RESOURCE DISK NOW!

Now is the time to store your original *Windows Student Resource Disk* in a safe place. If anything happens to your *Backup Resource Disk*, you can make another copy if you have your original *Windows Student Resource Disk*, following the steps shown in this tutorial.

2 Click to label the disk.

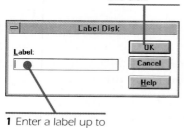

1 Enter a label up to 11 characters long.

LABELING DISKS

You can label each of your disks so its name appears above the contents list when you are using File Manager. To change a disk's label or add a label to a disk that hasn't already been labeled, pull down the **Disk** menu and click the **Label Disk** command to display a dialog box. Type the name of the disk into the **Label** text box (up to 11 characters) and then click the **OK** command button.

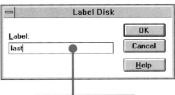

The text box displays the current name of the disk.

Type your last name into the text box.

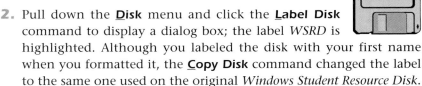

▶▶ TUTORIAL

1. Insert the backup *Windows Student Resource Disk* into drive A and select that drive.

2. Pull down the **Disk** menu and click the **Label Disk** command to display a dialog box; the label *WSRD* is highlighted. Although you labeled the disk with your first name when you formatted it, the **Copy Disk** command changed the label to the same one used on the original *Windows Student Resource Disk*.

3. Type your last name (abbreviating it to 11 characters if necessary); as you do so, the first character you type deletes the entire previous entry.

4. Click the **OK** command button. Your last name is now the disk's label, and it is displayed at the top of the contents list.

SELECTING FILES IN THE CONTENTS LIST

To perform operations on files such as copying, renaming, or deleting, you must first select the files to be affected. When you select files, the number selected and their total size is indicated on the status bar. (You can turn the display of this bar on and off with the **Status Bar** command on the **Options** menu.)

POINTING AND CLICKING TO SELECT FILES

You can select any single file by clicking it. However, at times you want to *extend the selection* to more than one item in the contents list.

▶ To extend the selection over sequential files, click the first filename to select it, and then either hold down ⇧Shift while you click the last filename or hold down ⇧Shift and use the arrow keys to extend the highlight over sequential items in the list.

▶ To select nonsequential items, hold down Ctrl while you click each item. To cancel a selection, hold down Ctrl and click the item again.

▶ To select more than one sequential group, click the first filename to select it, and then hold down ⇧Shift while you either click the last filename or use the arrow keys to extend the highlight over sequential items in the list. To select the next group, hold down Ctrl while you click the first item. Then hold down Ctrl+⇧Shift while you click the last item.

▶ To select all files in the contents list window, click any filename, then press /. If you then want to unselect some files, hold down Ctrl and click each of them.

USING THE SELECT FILES COMMAND

To select files, pull down the **File** menu and click the **Select Files** command to display a dialog box. Enter a filename specification and click the **Select** command button to select the files or the **Deselect** command button to unselect them. Rectangular boxes in the contents list surround each of the files that match the filename specification you entered. Click the **Close** command button to return to the directory, and the selected files are highlighted.

1 Enter a filename specification.

2 Click to select files that match the filename specification in the **File(s)** text box.

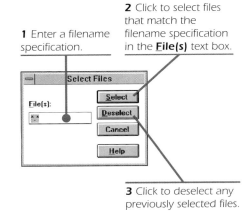

3 Click to deselect any previously selected files.

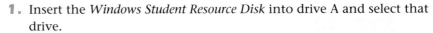

▶▶ TUTORIAL

Getting Ready

1. Insert the *Windows Student Resource Disk* into drive A and select that drive.

2. Double-click the *filemgr* directory on the directory tree to expand it and display its contents in the contents list.

Selecting All Files by Clicking

3. Click any filename in the contents list to select it.

4. Press ⌷ to select all of the files.

TIP: "MY SCREEN DOESN'T MATCH THE BOOK'S."

The default settings for File Manager display just the names of nonhidden files sorted by name. If your contents list is not displayed this way, your screen will not match the illustrations throughout this PicTorial. To make your screen match ours, pull down the **View** menu and:

▶ Click **By File Type**, then turn off **Show Hidden/System Files** and click the **OK** button

▶ Turn on the **Name** command

▶ Turn on the **Sort by Name** command

You will have to pull down the menu once for each setting you change.

1 Click any filename to select it.

2 Press ⌷ to select all files on the contents list.

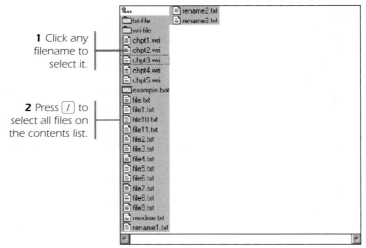

5. Hold down Ctrl and click the two subdirectories *txt-file* and *wri-file* (in the contents list) to unselect them.

Hold down Ctrl when you click the two directories to unselect them.

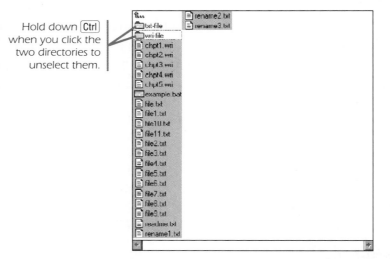

6. Click any filename to remove the highlight from all of the other files and select just the file you click.

Selecting Adjacent Files by Clicking

7. Click *chtp1.wri* to select it. Then hold down ⇧Shift and click *chpt5.wri* to select all adjacent files between it and the first file you selected.

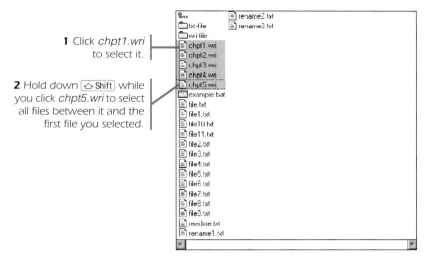

1 Click *chpt1.wri* to select it.

2 Hold down ⬆Shift while you click *chpt5.wri* to select all files between it and the first file you selected.

Selecting Nonadjacent Files by Clicking

8. Click *chpt1.wri* to select just it again. Then hold down Ctrl while you click *file1.txt* and *rename1.txt* to select these nonadjacent files.

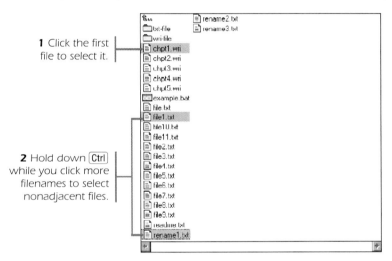

1 Click the first file to select it.

2 Hold down Ctrl while you click more filenames to select nonadjacent files.

9. Click the Up icon at the top of the contents list to remove the selection highlight from all of the files. (You may have to scroll it into view.)

Selecting All Files with the Menu

10. Pull down the **File** menu and click the **Select Files** command to display a dialog box. The *.* filename specification in the **Files(s)** text box means that all files will be selected.

11. Click the **Select** command button and then the **Close** command button to select all of the files.

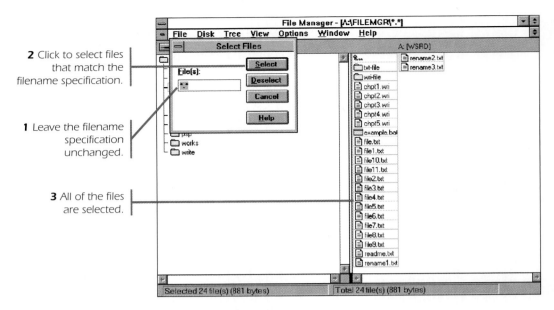

2 Click to select files that match the filename specification.

1 Leave the filename specification unchanged.

3 All of the files are selected.

Selecting Specific Files with the Menu

12. Pull down the **File** menu and click the **Select Files** command to display a dialog box. Click the **Deselect** command button to deselect all of the files on the contents list.

13. Type ***.txt** into the **File(s)** text box and click the **Select** command button to select all files with the *.txt* extension. The selected files are outlined on the contents list.

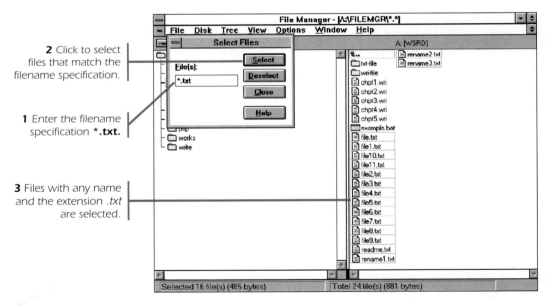

2 Click to select files that match the filename specification.

1 Enter the filename specification ***.txt.**

3 Files with any name and the extension *.txt* are selected.

14. Click the **Close** command button to close the dialog box. The selected files are highlighted.

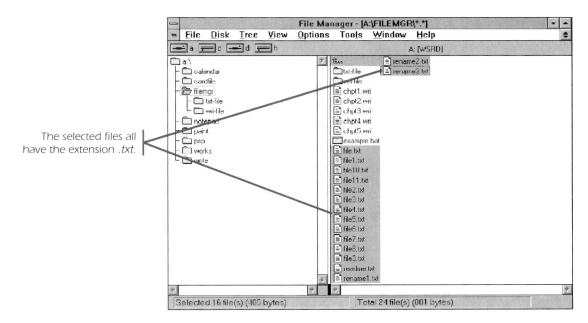

The selected files all have the extension *.txt*.

Finishing Up

15. Click the Up icon at the top of the contents list to remove the selection highlight from the files.

PAUSING FOR PRACTICE

Selecting files is a basic procedure that you must master to use File Manager. Pause here to continue selecting files on the contents list until you have mastered all of the selection procedures discussed in this section.

TURNING CONFIRMATION ON AND OFF

When you copy, move, and delete files, it's easy to accidentally overwrite an existing file of the same name or delete a file by mistake. To prevent such accidents, you can turn confirmation on. Then if the destination has a file of the same name, you are prompted to confirm that you want to replace it. If you are copying or moving a number of files, you can turn the prompt off for all files at once by choosing the **Yes To All** command button when the confirmation box appears.

To turn confirmation on, pull down the **Options** menu and click the **Confirmation** command to display a dialog box. Turn check boxes on for those actions where you want Windows to prompt you for confirmation. It is a good idea to leave all of these options on until you become an experienced Windows user.

Prompts when you delete a file

Prompts when you delete a directory

Prompts when you drag and drop a file

Prompts when you format or copy a disk

Prompts when you copy or move a file into a directory where a file already has the same name

1. Pull down the **Options** menu and click the **Confirmation** command to display a dialog box.

2. Turn on all confirmation options if they are not already on and then click the **OK** command button to return to the directory window. (If all the options are already on, click the **Cancel** command button.)

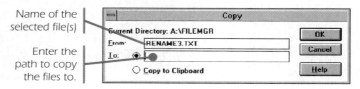

Confirmation
Confirm On
☒ File **D**elete
☒ **D**irectory Delete
☒ File **R**eplace
☒ **M**ouse Action
☒ Dis**k** Commands
OK
Cancel
Help

Turn on all confirmation options.

COPYING AND MOVING FILES WITH MENU COMMANDS

You can copy or move files or directories between drives or between directories. To copy or move more than one file or directory in a single procedure, select them first. The location you copy or move them from is called the *source*, and the location you copy or move them to is called the *destination*.

To copy or move files using menu commands, you first select them on the contents list, then pull down the **File** menu and click the **Copy** command. When the dialog box appears, you specify the *path* to where you want the file copied in the **To** text box. For example, to copy a file from drive B to drive A, you would enter the path **a:** or **a:** in the **To** text box. However, when a disk is divided into directories, you must specify not only a drive but also a directory. Specifying the drive and directories is called specifying a path.

Name of the selected file(s)

Enter the path to copy the files to.

Copy
Current Directory: A:\FILEMGR
From: RENAME3.TXT
To: ⊙
○ **C**opy to Clipboard
OK
Cancel
Help

Paths are simply a listing of the directories and subdirectories that specify exactly where a file is to be copied to. It is like telling someone to "file the letter to ACME Hardware in the manila folder labeled *ACME* in the hanging folder labeled *Hardware* in the third file cabinet from the right." These precise instructions make it easy to locate the file's destination.

To specify a path, you indicate the drive, then the name of all subdirectories leading to the destination. All elements must be separated from one another by backslashes (\)—for example, *a:\reports\markets*.

Drive identifier

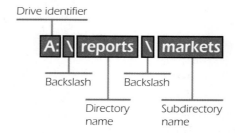

A: \ reports \ markets

Backslash   Backslash

Directory name   Subdirectory name

Let's assume your disk has the directories and files shown here:

Specify the path **a:** to copy or move files here.

Specify the path **a:\cardfile** to copy or move files here.

Specify the path **a:\filemgr\txt-file** to copy or move files here.

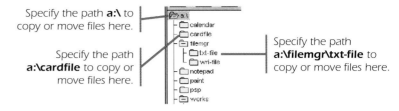

▶▶ TUTORIAL

Getting Ready

1. Insert the *Windows Student Resource* Disk into drive A and select that drive.

Copying Files

2. Click the *filemgr* directory on the directory tree to select it.

3. Click the file named *chpt1.wri* to select it on the contents list. Then hold down ⇧ Shift while you click the file named *chpt5.wri*. Release ⇧ Shift, and all of the files between *chpt1.wri* and *chpt5.wri* are selected.

All files with the extension *.wri* should be selected.

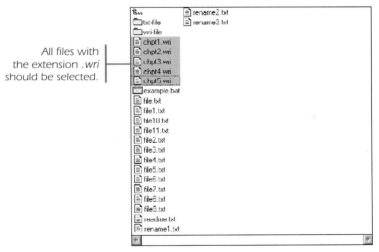

4. Pull down the **File** menu and click the **Copy** command to display a dialog box with the selected filenames displayed in the **From** text box.

All selected files are listed.

5. Type **a:\write** in the **To** text box.

Enter the path to copy the files to.

6. Click the **OK** command button to copy the files to the *write* directory. When copying is completed, the dialog box disappears.

7. Click the *write* directory on the directory tree to select it and see that the *chpt1.wri* through *chpt5.wri* files are now also listed in this directory.

Moving Files

8. Without changing directories, click the filename *chpt1.wri* in the contents list. Hold down ⇧Shift while you click the filename *chpt5.wri*, then release ⇧Shift. All of the files between *chpt1.wri* and *chpt5.wri* are selected.

The selected files ————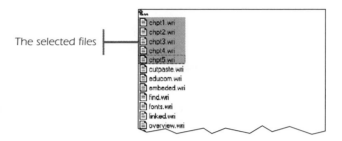

9. Pull down the **File** menu and click the **Move** command to display a dialog box with the selected files' names displayed in the **From** text box.

All selected files are listed. ————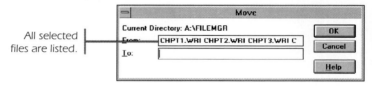

10. Type **a:\filemgr** in the **To** text box.

Enter the path to move the files to. ————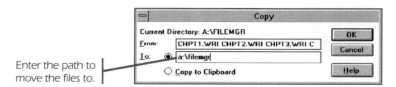

11. Click the **OK** command button to move the files to the *filemgr* directory. Since a copy already exists in the *filemgr* directory, the Confirm File Replace dialog box appears. Notice how information is supplied for both files so you can tell one from the other. In this case they are identical.

Information on the file you will replace

Information on the file you will replace it with ————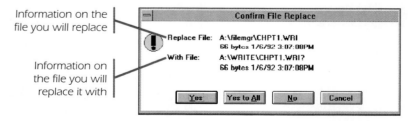

12. Click the **Yes** command button to move the file anyway. After it has been moved, the Confirm File Replace dialog box appears again, listing the next file.

13. Click the **Yes to All** command button to move all of the files into the directory. After the files have been moved, notice how they are no longer listed in the contents list for the *write* directory.

The *chpt1.wri* through *chpt5.wri* files are no longer listed because they have been moved to the *filemgr* directory.

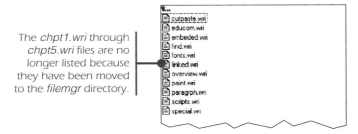

14. Click the *filemgr* directory on the directory tree to see the files listed in this directory. The files you moved overwrote the previous versions in the directory.

COPYING AND MOVING FILES BY DRAGGING AND DROPPING

Instead of using the menu to copy or move files, you can drag their file icons from one place to another with the mouse and then release them. This is called *dragging and dropping* and is a quick way to copy or move files.

As you drag files and directories, the mouse pointer assumes the shape of a file icon. If you drop the files onto a drive icon, they are copied or moved into the currently selected directory on that drive. To copy or move files into a specific directory, drop them onto the desired directory on the directory tree.

To drag and drop files and directories, follow these procedures:

1. Make sure both the source and destination are visible in the directory window or windows. (You can use the **Window** menu's **Cascade** or **Tile** command to do this.)

2. Select the files to be copied or moved.

3. Drag the files or directories to the destination's drive icon, directory window, or directory icon as follows:

▶ To move them to another location on the same disk, drag them there and release the mouse button to drop them.

▶ To move them to another disk, hold down ⬆Shift while dragging them. To drop them, release the mouse button and then release ⬆Shift.

▶ To copy them to another location on the same disk, hold down Ctrl while dragging them. To drop them, release the mouse button and then release Ctrl.

▶ To copy them to another disk, drag them there and release the mouse button to drop them.

4. If a confirmation box appears, read it and choose the appropriate option.

COMMON WRONG TURNS:
RELEASING ⇧Shift OR Ctrl TOO EARLY

Be careful when using the ⇧Shift or Ctrl keys while dragging. If you release these keys before you release the mouse button, the file will be copied instead of moved or moved instead of copied. If you have turned confirmation on for mouse actions, a dialog box will ask you to confirm the action and tell you whether the files are being copied or moved. If you released the key by mistake, just click the **Cancel** command button and try again.

▶▶ TUTORIAL

Getting Ready

1. Insert the *Windows Student Resource Disk* Disk into drive A and select that drive.

2. Click the *filemgr* directory on the directory tree to select it.

Selecting Files

3. Click the filename *file.txt* to select it.

4. Hold down ⇧Shift while you click the filename *rename3.txt*.

5. Release ⇧Shift, and all of the files between *file.txt* and *rename3.txt* are selected.

Copying Files

6. Hold down Ctrl, point anywhere in the selected files, and hold down the left mouse button. Drag the files (they are represented by a file icon) to the directory *notepad* on the directory tree.

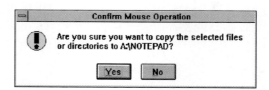

Adjacent files are selected.

The notepad directory is selected when you drag the file icon near it.

7. First release the mouse button and then release Ctrl. The Confirm Mouse Operation dialog box appears asking if you want to copy the files.

Confirm Mouse Operation

⚠ Are you sure you want to copy the selected files or directories to A:\NOTEPAD?

[Yes]   [No]

---

8. Click the **Yes** command button to copy the files. After the files have been copied, the dialog box disappears.

9. Click the *notepad* directory on the directory tree to see that the files have been copied there.

Selecting Files

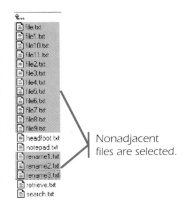

10. Click the filename *file.txt* to select it.

11. Hold down `⇧Shift` while you click the filename *file9.txt*, and then release `⇧Shift`. All of the files between *file.txt* and *file9.txt* are selected.

12. Hold down `Ctrl` while you click the filenames *rename1.txt*, *rename2.txt*, and *rename3.txt*, and then release `Ctrl`. This selects the nonadjacent file while leaving the first group selected.

Nonadjacent files are selected.

Moving Files

The *filemgr* directory is selected when you drag the file icon near it.

13. Hold down the left mouse button and drag the files to the directory *filemgr* on the directory tree.

14. Release the mouse button, and the Confirm Mouse Operation dialog box appears asking if you want to move the files.

15. Click the **Yes** command button to move the files. Since a copy already exists in the *filemgr* directory, the Confirm File Replace dialog box appears. Notice how information is supplied for both files so you can tell one from the other. In this case they are identical.

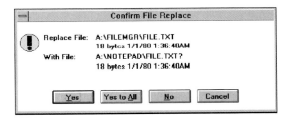

16. Click the **Yes** command button to move the file anyway. After it has been moved, the Confirm File Replace dialog box appears again, listing the next file.

17. Click the **Yes to All** command button to move all of the files into the *filemgr* directory. The files are no longer listed in the *notepad* directory.

CREATING DIRECTORIES

To organize your work on a hard disk drive, you create directories. When the directories are no longer needed, you remove them. When creating directories, you should have some kind of plan.

▶ Keep only essential files in the root directory.

▸ Store all program files related to a program in their own directory. For example, you might want separate directories for word processing, spreadsheet, and database applications.

▸ Do not store the data files that you create in the same directory as the program files. For example, the Microsoft Write program files might be in the Windows directory but you might store its document files in a directory named *write*.

▸ Keep all related data files in their own directories. For example, you might have separate directories for memos, letters, reports, financial documents, and name and address lists.

▸ Do not create too many levels of directories, since it takes time to specify them. Most disks can be well organized with no more than three levels, including the root directory.

When you first begin using a computer, directories may not seem important. However, after a while you will have so many files that if they aren't organized into directories, you'll have trouble knowing which file is which.

To copy or move files into a directory that does not exist, you first have to create the directory. To do so, select the directory in which you want the new directory to appear. For example, if you select the root directory, the new directory will be created one level below it. If you select an existing directory such as *letters*, the new directory will be a subdirectory of that directory. For example, to create the directories shown here: you would follow these procedures:

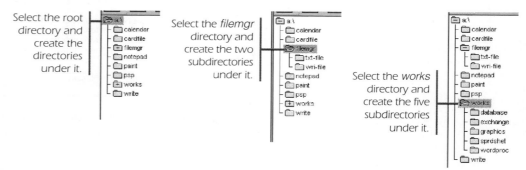

1. Select the root directory and create the first level of directories.

2. Select the *filemgr* directory and create the two subdirectories named *txt-file* and *wri-file*.

3. Select the *works* directory and create the five subdirectories named *database*, *exchange*, *graphics*, *sprdshet*, and *wordproc*.

Once you have selected the directory in which you want to create a subdirectory, pull down the **File** menu and click the **Create Directory** command to display a dialog box. Type the name of the new directory into the **Name** text box and then click the **OK** command button. Directory names follow the same conventions that you use for filenames. However, you should not use a period and extension, or you might confuse directories with filenames at some later date. Files and

The directory in which the new directory will be created

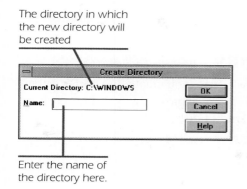

Enter the name of the directory here.

subdirectories in one directory can have the same names as files and subdirectories in other directories. If you want to create the new directory elsewhere on the disk, you can type a path in front of it. For example, to create a subdirectory named *new* in the directory named letters, type **c:\letters\new** into the **Name** text box.

▶▶ TUTORIAL

Getting Ready

1. Insert the *Windows Student Resource Disk* into drive A and select that drive.

Creating a Directory

2. Click the root directory, *a:*, on the directory tree to select it.

3. Pull down the **File** menu and click the **Create Directory** command to display a dialog box.

4. Type **backups** in the **Name** text box.

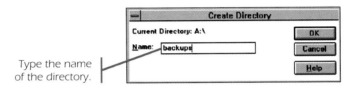

Type the name of the directory.

5. Click the **OK** command button to create a directory named *backups*. The new directory is now listed on the directory tree.

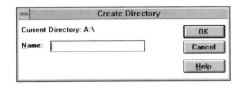

The new directory is listed on the tree.

Creating Subdirectories

6. Click the *backups* directory on the directory tree to select it.

7. Pull down the **File** menu and click the **Create Directory** command to display a dialog box.

8. Type **chpts** in the **Name** text box.

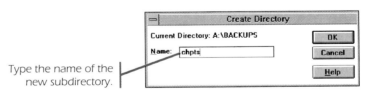

Type the name of the new subdirectory.

9. Click the **OK** command button to create a subdirectory named *chpts* in the directory named *backups*.

10. Pull down the **File** menu and click the **Create Directory** command to display a dialog box.

11. Type **others** in the **Name** text box.

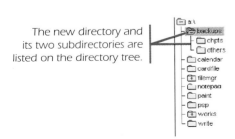

The new directory and its two subdirectories are listed on the directory tree.

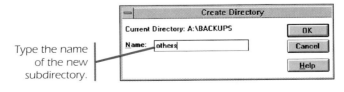

Type the name of the new subdirectory.

12. Click the **OK** command button to create a subdirectory named *others* in the directory named *backups*. Your directory tree should now look like the illustration at the left.

Moving Files into the New Chpts Subdirectory

13. Click the *filemgr* directory on the directory tree to select it.

14. Select all of the files in the contents list that have the name *chpt*.

15. Drag the files to the new subdirectory *chpts* on the directory tree and release the mouse button. The Confirm Mouse Operation dialog box appears asking if you want to move the files.

16. Click the **Yes** command button to move the files.

17. Click the *chpts* subdirectory on the directory tree to see that the files have been moved there.

Moving Files into the New Others Subdirectory

18. Click the *filemgr* directory on the directory tree to select it.

19. Select the remaining file(s) in the contents list but don't select the subdirectories *wri-file* and *txt-file*.

20. Drag the file(s) to the subdirectory *others* on the directory tree and release the mouse button. The Confirm Mouse Operation dialog box appears asking if you want to move the files.

21. Click the **Yes** command button to move the files. When the move operation is completed, the *filemgr* directory contains only the subdirectories *wri-file* and *txt-file* and the file *hidden.txt*, which is not displayed.

22. Click the *others* subdirectory on the directory tree to see that the files have been copied there.

DELETING FILES AND DIRECTORIES

To delete unneeded files or directories from your disk, you first select them and then use **Delete** command on the **File** menu. To remove a directory, first select it on the directory tree. Then pull down the **File** menu and click the **Delete** command to display a confirmation box.

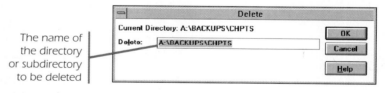

The name of the directory or subdirectory to be deleted

If the directory you are deleting contains files, a second directory box appears.

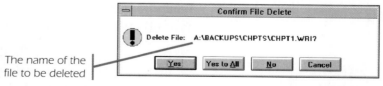

The name of the file to be deleted

When deleting files and directories, you should always have **File Delete** and **Directory Delete** confirmations turned on so you are prompted to confirm any deletions. Once the confirmation box appears, if you are deleting a number of files and directories, you can turn the prompt off for each deletion by choosing the **Yes To All** command button.

TIP: UNDELETING FILES

If you are using DOS 5 or later versions, you can often recover or "undelete" files should you delete them by mistake. With DOS 5 you use the *undelete* command from the DOS command prompt. With DOS 6, you open the Microsoft Tools group window and double-click the Undelete application icon. There are also programs available from other publishers that will recover many lost files for you.

▶▶ **TUTORIAL**

Getting Ready

1. Insert the *Windows Student Resource Disk* into drive A and select that drive.

Deleting a Directory

2. Click the subdirectory *chpts* on the directory tree (under the new *backups* directory) to select it.

3. Pull down the **File** menu and click the **Delete** command to display a dialog box listing the path to the current directory in the Delete text box.

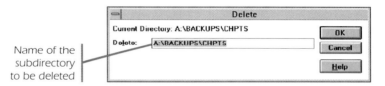

Name of the subdirectory to be deleted

4. Click the **OK** command button to begin deleting, and the Confirm Directory Delete dialog box is displayed.

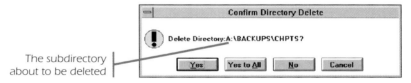

The subdirectory about to be deleted

5. Click the **Yes** command button to confirm that you want to delete the directory, and the Confirm File Delete box appears and lists the first file in the directory to be deleted.

The name of the first file to be deleted

Click to delete all without further confirmation.

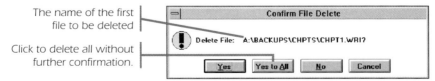

6. Click the **Yes to All** command button to confirm that you want to delete all of the files in the directory. In a moment, the subdirectory *chpts* is no longer listed on the directory tree.

Deleting a File

7. Click the *others* directory on the directory tree to select it.

8. Click the filename *example.bat* on the contents list to select it.

9. Pull down the **File** menu and click the **Delete** command to display the Delete dialog box listing the selected file.

10. Click the **OK** command button to delete the file, and the Confirm File Delete dialog box appears listing the selected file.

11. Click the **Yes** command button to delete the listed file, and it is no longer listed on the contents list.

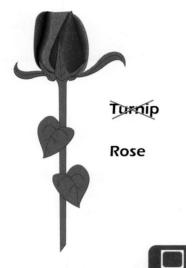

Turnip

Rose

RENAMING FILES AND DIRECTORIES

To rename files or directories, you use the **Rename** command on the **File** menu. Don't rename any of the directories or files associated with Windows and its applications. If you do so, the application may not be able to find the files that it needs to run correctly.

When you click the **Rename** command, a dialog box appears with the current name listed in the **From** text box. Type the new name into the **To** text box and click the **OK** command button.

To rename groups of files, you can use wildcards. For example, to rename all *.bak* files to *.doc*, you would enter **.bak* in the **From** box and **.doc* in the **To** box.

TIP: CONTENTS LIST ISN'T ACCURATE

When you change disks in a drive or when you copy, move, rename, or delete files, the contents list is not always updated. To be sure the current files are listed, always pull down the **Window** menu and click the **Refresh** command to update the directory of the disk.

▶▶ **TUTORIAL**

Getting Ready

1. Insert the *Windows Student Resource Disk* into drive A and select that drive.

Renaming a Directory

2. Click the *backups* directory on the directory tree to select it.

3. Pull down the **File** menu and click the **Rename** command to display a dialog box. The current name is displayed in the **From** text box.

The name of the selected directory

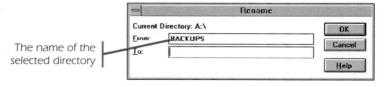

4. Type **newfiles** into the **To** text box.

The new name for the directory

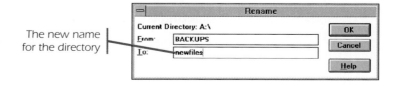

5. Click the **OK** command button to rename the directory. The new name is now listed on the directory tree.

Renaming a File

6. Click the *notepad* directory on the directory tree to select it.

7. Click the *retrieve.txt* file on the contents list to select it.

8. Pull down the **File** menu and click the **Rename** command to display a dialog box. The current name is displayed in the **From** text box.

The name of the selected file

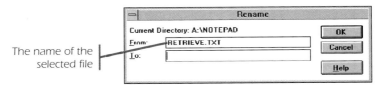

9. Type **newfile.txt** into the **To** text box.

The new name for the file

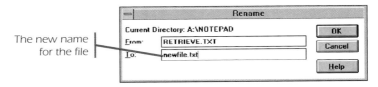

10. Click the **OK** command button to rename the file.

SEARCHING FOR A FILE OR DIRECTORY

You pull down the **File** menu and click the **Search** command to locate files and directories on a disk. When you choose this command, the Search dialog box is displayed with the wildcards *.* in the **Search** For box and the current directory in the **Start From** box.

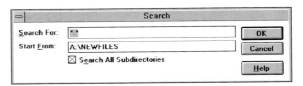

To locate files or directories, enter a filename specification in the **Search For** box. For example, to find all back copies of documents, you might enter *.*bak*.

To search all subdirectories in the current directory, turn on the **Search All Subdirectories** check box. If you want to search only the current directory, turn the check box off.

To begin the search, click the **OK** command button. (You can press [Esc] at any point to stop the search.) When the search is completed, the Search Results box is displayed listing all of the files and directories that matched your filename specification.

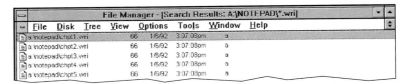

▶▶ TUTORIAL

1. Insert the *Windows Student Resource Disk* into drive A and select that drive.

2. Pull down the **Window** menu and click the **Refresh** command to update the directory window.

3. Click the *a:* directory on the directory tree to select it.

4. Pull down the **File** menu and click the **Search** command to display a dialog box.

  ▶ The filename specification **.** is listed in the **Search For** text box.

  ▶ *A:* is the directory listed in the **Start From** text box.

  ▶ The **Search All Subdirectories** check box is turned on.

5. Type **newfile.txt** into the **Search For** text box and click the **OK** command button. The Search Results screen is displayed, showing *a:\notepad\newfile.txt*.

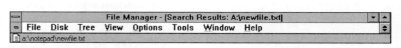

6. Double-click the Search window's Control-menu box to close the window.

▶▶ SKILL-BUILDING EXERCISES

1. Formatting Additional Data Disks

Format any additional data disks that you might need for your own work.

2. Checking Disk Labels

Use the File Manager to display the disk label for each of your floppy disks. If you find any disk with a name, write it down.

3. Specifying Your System's Disks

List the specifications for the disks your system requires in the spaces below. You will find this information in the manual that accompanies the computer. Look up "*disks*"

Specification	Your System's Disks
Disk size	_____
Number of sides	_____
Density	_____
Storage capacity	_____

or "*disk drives*" in the index, and refer to the listed sections. If you cannot find the information in the manual, refer to the specifications printed on the box that your disks came in.

4. **Searching for Files and Directories**

Use the **Searc̲h̲** command on **F̲ile** menu to locate the files listed below. Next to each file that you find, list the path displayed on the Search Results screen.

Filename	Path
search.txt	_____
educom.wri	_____
doorway.bmp	_____
setup.exe	_____
phonelst.crd	_____
classes.cal	_____
building.bmp	_____

PicTorial **4** ▶VISualQuiz

1. This illustration shows two 3½-inch floppy disks. Describe what the cutouts on each tell you about the disks.

a. _____

b. _____

2. This illustration shows the dialog box that appears when you select the **Format Disk** command from the **Disk** menu. Explain when you would change the settings for a and b and when you would turn on the check box c.

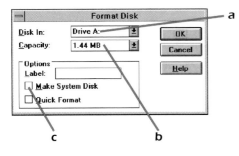

a. _____

b. _____

c. _____

3. Describe two ways you would select the files shown selected in this illustration of the contents list.

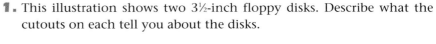

_____

_____

4. Describe how you would select the files shown selected in this illustration of the contents list.

_____

_____

5. Describe what happens when each of these check boxes is turned on.

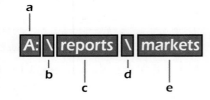

a. _____

b. _____

c. _____

d. _____

e. _____

6. List the name of each of the labeled parts of this path.

a. _____

b. _____

c. _____

d. _____

e. _____

Where would a file be copied to if you specified this path in the **To** text box of the dialog box that is displayed when copying a file?

_____

7. Indicate the path that you would enter into the **To** text box to copy a file to the labeled directories.

a. _____

b. _____

c. _____

d. _____

e. _____

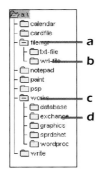

8. List the directories you would select before creating each of the labeled directories or subdirectories.

a. _____

b. _____

c. _____

d. _____

9. This illustration shows the box that appears when you are deleting files if confirmation is on. Describe what happens if you click each of the labeled buttons when the first file is listed.

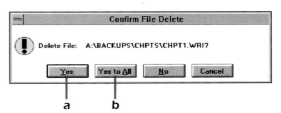

a. _____

b. _____

True-False (Circle T if the statement is true or F if it is false.)

T   F   **1.** To change the selected drive, you double-click one of the drive icons.

T   F   **2.** You can drag the split bar the separates the directory tree from the contents list so one window has more space.

T   F   **3.** The topmost directory on the directory tree is called the *root directory*.

T   F   **4.** To select a directory, you just click its name or icon on the directory tree.

T   F   **5.** To expand a directory, you double-click its name or icon on the directory tree.

T   F   **6.** To display only selected files, you pull down the **View** menu and click the **By File Type** command to display a dialog box.

T   F   **7.** The filename specification **.doc* will display files with any name as long as they have the extension *.doc*.

T   F   **8.** The filename specification *c??t.txt* will display the files named *coot* and *coat* if they have the extension *.txt*.

T   F   **9.** If you have more than one directory window open, you can tile or cascade them.

T   F   **10.** Tiled directory windows don't overlap and cascaded windows do.

T   F   **11.** When formatting a data disk, Windows automatically formats the disk in drive A to the capacity of that drive unless you specify otherwise.

T   F   **12.** When formatting 3½-inch floppy disks, you can tell a disk's capacity by its cutouts. For example, a 1.44MB disk has one cutout.

T   F   **13.** When formatting a disk, you turn on the **Make System Disk** check box only if you want to be able to boot the computer from the disk you are formatting.

T   F   **14.** As long as the disk in drive A is a system disk, it doesn't matter whether you boot from drive A or drive C.

T   F   **15.** To make a duplicate copy of a disk, you can use either the **Copy** command on the **File** menu or the **Copy Disk** command on the **Disk** menu.

T   F   **16.** The best thing about the **Copy Disk** command on the **Disk** menu is that you can use it to copy between dissimilar disks or drives. For example, it works well between 3½- and 5¼-inch drives.

T   F   **17.** When you use the **Copy Disk** command on the **Disk** menu, the disk you are copying to doesn't need to be formatted.

T   F   **18.** You can only select files that are next to each other on the contents list.

T   F   **19.** To select all of the files on the contents list, you have to be patient and click them one at a time.

T F **20.** Turning confirmation on is a good way to help you avoid mistakes when deleting and copying files.

T F **21.** To copy a file named *john.doc* to the *letters* directory on drive C, you would enter the path *c:\letters* into the **To** text box when the dialog box appears.

T F **22.** When dragging a file to the same disk, hold down Ctrl or the file will be moved.

T F **23.** When dragging a file to a different disk, hold down Ctrl or the file will be copied.

T F **24.** When holding down Ctrl while dragging a file, you release Ctrl before the mouse button to drop the file.

T F **25.** When you create a new directory, you begin by selecting the directory on the directory tree under which you want the new directory to appear.

T F **26.** Before you can delete a directory, you must first delete all of the files that it contains.

T F **27.** Once you have deleted files or directories, it's impossible to recover them.

T F **28.** Sometimes the contents list isn't accurate—it doesn't list all of the files that it contains.

 Multiple Choice (Circle the correct answer.)

1. File Manager's directory window is normally divided into halves so the ___ can be displayed at the same time.

    a. Contents of two different drives

    b. Filenames and sizes

    c. Directory tree and contents list

    d. Directories and subdirectories

2. To display just the files on a disk, pull down the **View** menu and click the ___ command.

    a. **Tree and Directory**

    b. **Tree Only**

    c. **Directory Only**

    d. None of the above

3. To save any changes you make to File Manager's layout so they are in effect the next time you use the application, ___.

    a. Press Esc

    b. Pull down the **File** menu and click the **Save** command

    c. Press Alt + ⇧ Shift + F4

    d. None of the above

4. To change the selected drive, you click the drive's icon or ___.

    a. Hold down Ctrl while you press the drive's letter

    b. Press Tab⇆ to move the selection cursor to the drive icons, use the arrow keys to highlight the desired drive, and then press Enter ↵

   c. Pull down the **Disk** menu and click the **Select Drive** command to display a dialog box listing all of the drives on your system, then select the drive you want to change to and click the **OK** command button

   d. Any of the above

5. To expand a directory without creating a new directory window, you ___.

   a. Double-click the directory

   b. Click the directory

   c. Drag the directory to the contents list

   d. Pull down the **File** menu and click the **Open** command

6. To list just the filename and size on the contents list, you pull down the View menu and click the ___ command.

   a. **Sort by Si_z_e**

   b. **_N_ame**

   c. **Partial Details**

   d. **All File Details**

7. To display all files that begin with the letter _c_ and have an extension that begins with the letter _t_, you would pull down the **View** menu, click the **By File _T_ype** command, end enter ___ into the **_N_ame** text box.

   a. **c?.t?**

   b. **c.txt**

   c. **c*.t***

   d. None of the above

8. To open an existing file with an application program, you must know ___.

   a. The drive it's on, the directory it's in, and its filename

   b. What characters are legal in filenames

   c. The date and time it was created

   d. All of the above

9. To save a file the first time with an application program, you must specify ___.

   a. Its filename

   b. The drive it's to be stored on

   c. The directory it's to be saved in

   d. All of the above

10. When more than one directory window is open, you can switch among them by ___.

   a. Clicking anywhere on a window

   b. Pressing `Ctrl`+`Tab↹` or `Ctrl`+`F6`

   c. Pulling down the **_W_indow** menu and clicking the window's name

   d. Any of the above

11. To select adjacent files on the contents list, you ___.

   a. Click the first filename to select it, and then hold down `⇧ Shift` while you click the last filename

    b. Hold down ⇧Shift and use the arrow keys to extend the highlight

    c. Hold down Ctrl while you click each filename

    d. Any of the above

12. You can turn confirmation on so you are asked to confirm ___.

    a. Deleting files

    b. Deleting directories

    c. Replacing a file by another with the same name

    d. All of the above

13. To copy a file to the same disk by dragging and dropping, you must hold down ___ while dragging it.

    a. Ctrl

    b. Alt

    c. No key

    d. None of the above

14. To move a file to another disk by dragging and dropping, you must hold down ___ while dragging it.

    a. Ctrl

    b. Alt

    c. No key

    d. None of the above

15. To create a new subdirectory, you begin by selecting the directory ___ where you want the new one.

    a. Immediately below

    b. Immediately above

    c. On the same level as

    d. None of the above

Fill in the Blank (Enter your answer in the space provided.)

1. When you open File Manager, it displays the _____ which is divided into two parts. On the left is the _____ and on the right is the _____.

2. To change the selected drive you _____ one of the _____.

3. To save changes you make to File Manager, you can press _____.

4. The topmost directory is called the _____ directory.

5. When a directory contains other directories, they are called _____.

6. To arrange directory windows side by side so they don't overlap, you _____ them. To arrange them so they overlap one another, you _____.

7. To tile directory windows side by side, hold down _____ when you click/ the **Tile** command on the **Window** menu.

8. You can tell a 3½-inch floppy disk's capacity by its _____ since a 1.44MB disk has _____ and a 720KB disk has _____.

9. To make a duplicate copy of a disk, use the _____ command on the _____ menu.

10. To select a series of adjacent files on the contents list, you can click the first name and then hold down _____ while you click the last.

11. To select nonadjacent files on the contents list, you hold down _____ while you click each file.

12. To select all of the files on the contents list, you select one then press _____.

13 To copy a file named *john.doc* to the *letters* directory on drive C, you would enter the path _____ into the **To** text box when the dialog box appears.

14. To ensure that the contents list lists all of the files that it contains, you should pull down the Window menu and click the _____ command.

15. When dragging a file to another location on the same disk, it is normally _____. When dragging it to another disk, it is normally _____.

16. When dragging a file to another location on the same disk, hold down _____ to copy it. When dragging it to another disk, hold down _____ to move it.

17. When copying a file to another location on the same drive, be sure to release _____ before releasing _____.

18. When moving a file to another location on a different disk, be sure to release _____ before releasing _____.

19. To tile or cascade directory windows, you pull down the _____ menu and click the _____ or _____ commands.

Projects

Project 1. Exploring the Directory Tree

Use File Manager to explore the directory tree of the hard disk on your system where Windows is stored. You should be able to locate a tree similar to the one shown in the figure shown here.

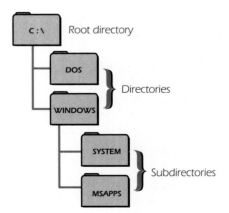

Project 2. Identifying File Icons

Display the contents list for the *Windows Student Resource Disk*, search the icons for an example of each type listed below, and write in its filename:

File Type	Filename
Directory	_____
Program file	_____
Document file associated with an application	_____
System or hidden file	_____
All other files	_____

Project 3. Creating and Deleting Directories

1. Insert the *Windows Student Resource Disk* into one of the disk drives and select that drive.
2. Create a directory named *1994*.
3. Create two subdirectories in the *1994* directory named *sales* and *budgets*.
4. Delete all the new directories and subdirectories from the disk.

Chapter 3
WORKING WITH APPLICATION PROGRAMS

<table>
<tr>
<td>

PicTorial 5

WORKING WITH NOTEPAD, PRINT MANAGER, AND THE CLIPBOARD

</td>
<td>

After completing this PicTorial, you will be able to:

▶ Start applications from Program Manager

▶ Exit applications and return to Program Manager

▶ Open existing documents

▶ Enter and edit text

▶ Save documents and clear the screen

▶ Print documents and manage print jobs with Print Manager

▶ Copy and move text and view data on the Clipboard

</td>
</tr>
</table>

The primary purpose of Windows is to make it easy to open and operate applications, including those supplied with Windows. Windows-supplied applications include those in the Main group such as File Manager and Control Panel and those in the Accessories group such as Write, Paintbrush, and Notepad. When you work with many applications such as these, you create *documents*—the generic term that Windows uses for any file of data. Using menu commands, you can also *save* these documents on a disk for later use and *open*, or retrieve, previously saved documents. If you want to file a document or distribute it to others, you can print it.

In this PicTorial you'll use the Notepad application to open, edit, save, and print documents, and to copy and move data. You'll also be introduced to two other essential Windows applications—Print Manager, which you use to manage print jobs; and the Clipboard, which you use to cut and paste data within or between applications. We're using Notepad to introduce basic concepts because it is one of the simplest Windows applications and won't confuse you while you learn procedures and techniques that apply to all other Windows applications.

STARTING AND EXITING APPLICATIONS

Starting (or opening or *launching*) a Windows application is as easy as double-clicking its icon. When you are finished with an application, you can close or quit or exit it. This removes it from the computer's memory and removes its window or icon from the desktop (although its icon remains in the group window). To close, or exit, an open application, do one of the following:

▶ Pull down the application's **File** menu and click the **Exit** command.

▶ Click the application's Control-menu box to display the Control menu and then click the **Close** command.

▶ Double-click the application's Control-menu box.

▶ Make it the active window and press Alt + F4 .

If you try to close an application without saving changes to your document, a dialog box asks if you want to save the current changes. Click the **Yes** command button to save the document or the **No** command button to abandon it. To return to the application instead of closing it, click the **Cancel** command button.

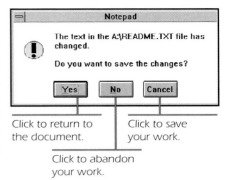

Click to return to the document.

Click to abandon your work.

Click to save your work.

TIP: APPLICATIONS RUNNING AS ICONS

Windows allows you to specify whether an application runs in a window or as an icon when you first open it. If the application is set up to run as an icon, double-clicking its icon in a group window loads it into the computer's memory and then displays it as an icon on the desktop. (You can also display an application this way at any time by clicking its Minimize button.) To open an application that is running as an icon, double-click its icon on the desktop.

▶▶ TUTORIAL

1. Load Windows so that Program Manager is displayed.
2. Open the Accessories group window.

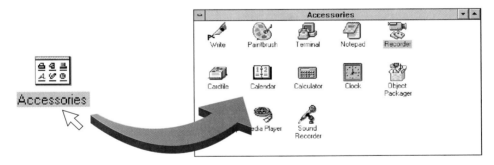

3. Double-click Notepad's icon to open the application.

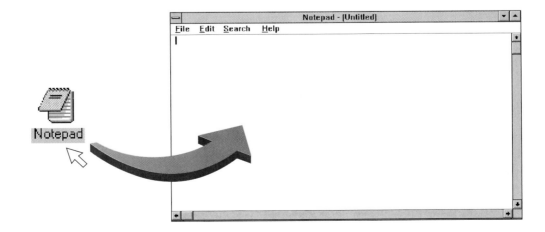

4. Pull down the **File** menu and click the **Exit** command to close the application.

1 Pull down the menu.

2 Click to close the application.

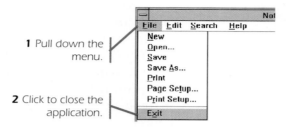

5. Double-click Notepad's icon to open the application again.

6. Click Notepad's Control-menu box to display the Control menu, and then click the **Close** command to close the application.

1 Click to display the Control menu.

2 Click to close the application.

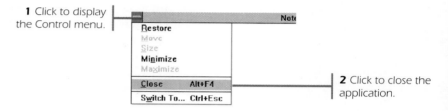

Double-click to close the application.

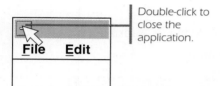

7. Double-click Notepad's icon to open the application again.

8. Double-click Notepad's Control-menu box to close the application.

9. Double-click Notepad's icon to open the application again.

10. Press Alt + F4 to close the application.

11. Double-click Notepad's icon to open the application again.

PAUSING FOR PRACTICE

Opening and closing applications is a basic skill and is the same for all applications. Pause here and continue practicing the various ways you can close an application until you have mastered them.

UNDERSTANDING THE NOTEPAD SCREEN

When you first load Notepad, its document screen is empty except for a flashing vertical line called the insertion point. Look closely at the window and you'll see many of the elements you have already learned about.

▶   The Control-menu box is in the upper-left corner.

▶   The title bar lists the application's name (Notepad) and the document's name (Untitled until you save it).

▶   The Minimize and Maximize buttons are in the upper-right corner.

▶   The menu bar lists the names of Notepad's menus.

▶   Scroll bars are on the right and bottom sides of the window.

▶   The insertion point is a flashing vertical line.

▶ The mouse pointer takes on the shape of an I-beam in the large open area that contains the insertion point. As you'll soon see, this narrow shape allows you to accurately position the pointer between characters of text.

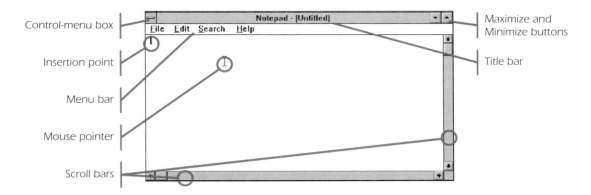

Control-menu box

Insertion point

Menu bar

Mouse pointer

Scroll bars

Maximize and Minimize buttons

Title bar

OPENING EXISTING DOCUMENTS

Notepad is a simple word processing application, called a text editor, that you can use to work with short documents. Notepad can only create and edit a special kind of document called a *text file* or *ASCII text file*. These documents contain just printable ASCII characters with little or no formatting information so they are easily exchanged between applications. Text files are normally identified by their *.txt* extension. This extension isn't essential, but it is a convention that is frequently followed.

To open an existing document, pull down the **File** menu and click the **Open** command. The Open dialog box that appears has four settings that you can select—the drive, the directory, the filename, and the file type.

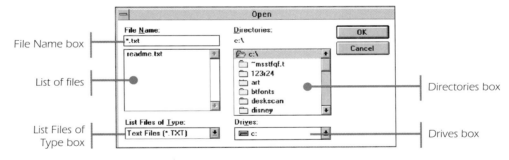

File Name box

List of files

List Files of Type box

Directories box

Drives box

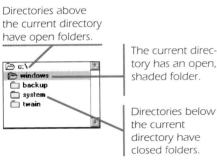

Directories above the current directory have open folders.

The current directory has an open, shaded folder.

Directories below the current directory have closed folders.

The currently selected drive is listed in the **Drives** drop-down list box. To change the drive, click the down arrow on the box to display a list of the drives on your system. Scroll the drive you want into view and click it to select it. When you do so, the listed directories and files change.

To list the document you want, it may also be necessary to change the directory. To do so, you need to understand the **Directories** list box.

Directories all have icons that look like file folders. The current directory, the one that is selected, has its folder open and shaded. The directory above the current one, if any, has an open, unshaded folder. The current directory's subdirectories, if any, have closed file folders. Slight indents also show which directory is above the current directory and which subdirectories are below it. Also, the current directory and the path to it are listed just below the heading **Directories**.

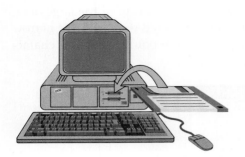

To select a new directory, double-click its name in the **Directories** list box. Doing so allows you to quickly move up or down levels.

When you change drives or directories, the list of documents displayed in the list of files box changes. If no documents are displayed there, it doesn't mean there are none; it just means that the list box displays only documents with the extension *.txt*. This is because the filename specification in the **File Name** text box is **.txt*. To list all documents, you could type ***.*** and press Enter↵ or you could display the **List Files of Type** drop-down list box and click the **All Files [*.*]** command.

When you click a filename in the list of files to select it, its name is displayed in the **File Name** text box. You then click the **OK** command button, and the computer copies the document from the disk into the computer's memory so that it can be displayed on the screen and edited. The copy of the document on the disk remains unchanged until you save the document again.

COMMON WRONG TURNS: DIRECTORY ISN'T LISTED

If the directory you want to select isn't listed in the **Directories** list box, the chances are you have to move up one or more levels to see it. Double-click the first directory above the current one to display its directories. If the one you want still isn't listed, double-click the first directory above the current one and so on until you find the directory you are looking for.

▶▶ TUTORIAL

Getting Ready

1. If Notepad isn't open, open the Accessories group and double-click the Notepad icon. Click Notepad's Maximize button to display the application at full screen.

2. Insert your *Windows Student Resource Disk* into drive A.

3. Pull down Notepad's **File** menu and click the **Open** command to display the Open dialog box that we have just been examining.

Specifying a Drive

4. Click the **Drives** box's down arrow to display a drop-down list of the drives on your system.

5. Click *a:* to select it and list it in the **Drives** box (you may have to click the up scroll arrow to see it before you can click it).

 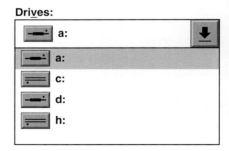

Specifying a Directory

6. Double-click the *notepad* directory in the **Directories** list box. This does two things:

▶ The directory changes to *notepad* and the path *a:\notepad* is shown above the list box.

▶ The documents in the directory with the extension *.txt* are displayed in the list of files.

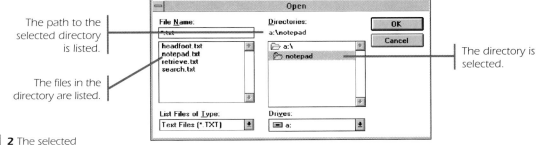

The path to the selected directory is listed.

The files in the directory are listed.

The directory is selected.

2 The selected file is listed in the text box.

1 Click to select.

Opening a Document

7. Click the *notepad.txt* filename in the list of files to select it and display its name in the **File Name** text box.

LOOKING BACK: WILDCARDS

The reason only files with the extension *.txt* are displayed is that the **File Name** text box contains the characters **.txt*. The asterisk is a wildcard standing for any filename, and *.txt* specifies the file's extension. To Windows the line reads "display files with any name but they must have the extension *.txt.*"

8. Click the **OK** command button to open the document.

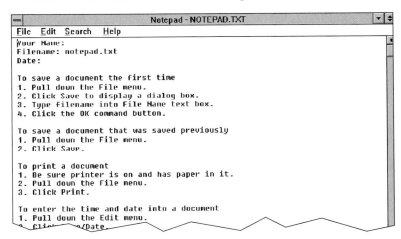

Moving Around the Document

9. Press <kbd>PgDn</kbd> a few times to page down through the document.

10. Press <kbd>PgUp</kbd> a few times to page up through the document.

11. Use the scroll bar to explore the document.

LOOKING BACK: USING SCROLL BARS

▶ Click the up or down scroll arrows to scroll a line at a time.

▶ Click above or below the scroll box to scroll a screen at a time.

▶ Point to the up or down scroll arrows and hold down the left mouse button to scroll continuously.

▶ Drag the scroll box up or down the scroll bar to scroll to a specific place in the document.

Finishing Up

12. Pull down the **File** menu and click the **New** command to clear the screen.

PAUSING FOR PRACTICE

Opening documents and clearing the screen are basic skills. Pause here to practice opening the *notepad.txt* file in the *notepad* directory and the *readme.txt* file in the root directory until you have the procedure memorized.

ENTERING AND EDITING TEXT

Notepad is a very simple application with a limited number of commands. To use it with your own documents, all you have to know is how to move the insertion point and enter or delete text.

As you enter text with Notepad, lines normally continue past the right edge of the window until you press <kbd>Enter ←</kbd>. In this way, it is much like typing on a typewriter. However, to make lines automatically end when they reach the right edge of the window, you can turn on *word wrap*. With word wrap on, when a word cannot fit at the end of a line without continuing past the right edge of the window, it automatically moves, or "wraps," to the beginning of the next line. The length of the lines in the window does not reflect their length when printed. But lines longer than the page width may have words split in the middle at the right margin, or lines on the printout may be of uneven length. As you will see later, the margins and line length on the printout are controlled by the **Print Setup** command on the **File** menu.

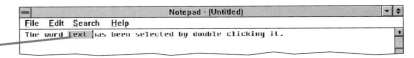

If a word extends past the right edge of the window

If a word extends past the right edge of the window it wraps to the next line.

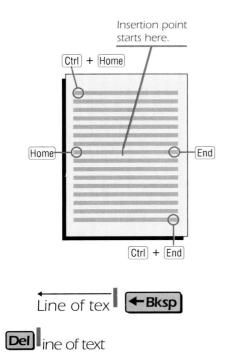

Insertion point starts here.

Ctrl + Home

Home   End

Ctrl + End

Line of tex ◄ Bksp

Del line of text

The insertion point moves automatically as you enter text and always indicates where the next character you type will appear. However, to insert or delete text, you can move the insertion point to any place in the document. To move the insertion point with the mouse, point to where you want to move it and click. This moves the insertion point to where the mouse pointer is. You can also move the insertion point a character or line at a time with the arrow keys. To move in big jumps, you can press Home or End to move it to the beginning or end of a line. If you hold down Ctrl when you press either of these keys, the insertion point moves to the beginning or end of the document.

To delete text, you press ◄ Bksp or Del. Pressing ◄ Bksp moves the insertion point to the left, deleting characters as it moves. Pressing Del leaves the insertion point where it is, but draws the line of text to its right toward it, deleting characters as the line moves. If you hold either of these keys down, they rapidly delete one character after another.

To delete words, phrases, or even larger sections, it is faster to select them first. To select a word, double-click it.

A word is selected by double-clicking it.

| Notepad - (Untitled) |
| File Edit Search Help |
| The word Text has been selected by double clicking it. |

To select larger sections, point to the first character to be selected. Then do either of the following:

▶ Hold down the left button, and drag the mouse to the right or down the screen to expand the highlight over adjacent text. When the text that you want to select is highlighted, release the left button and it remains highlighted.

▶ Hold down ⇧ Shift and press → to extend the highlight. When the text that you want to select is highlighted, release ⇧ Shift and it remains highlighted.

A phrase is selected by dragging the mouse pointer over it.

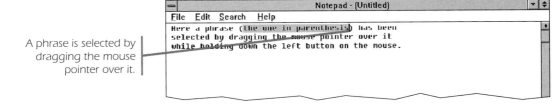

| Notepad - (Untitled) |
| File Edit Search Help |
| Here a phrase (the one in parenthesis) has been selected by dragging the mouse pointer over it while holding down the left button on the mouse. |

To select the entire document, pull down the **Edit** menu and click the **Select All** command. To remove the highlight from selected text, click anywhere in the window.

▶▶ TUTORIAL

1. Pull down Notepad's **Edit** menu and if the **Word Wrap** command does not have a check (✔) in front of it to indicate that it is on, click it to turn it on. If the command does have a check mark, click anywhere outside of the menu to close the menu.

Entering a Document

2. Type the document shown here. Press ⎣Enter↵⎦ at the end of each line where the symbol ⎣Enter↵⎦ is shown. If you make mistakes, delete them with ⎣← Bksp⎦ or leave them until later.

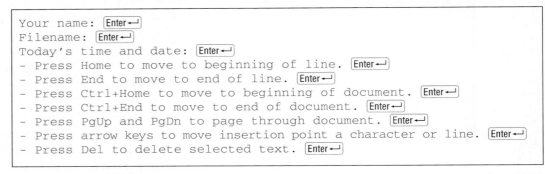

```
Your name: [Enter ↵]
Filename: [Enter ↵]
Today's time and date: [Enter ↵]
- Press Home to move to beginning of line. [Enter ↵]
- Press End to move to end of line. [Enter ↵]
- Press Ctrl+Home to move to beginning of document. [Enter ↵]
- Press Ctrl+End to move to end of document. [Enter ↵]
- Press PgUp and PgDn to page through document. [Enter ↵]
- Press arrow keys to move insertion point a character or line. [Enter ↵]
- Press Del to delete selected text. [Enter ↵]
```

Moving Through the Document

3. Use the arrow keys to move the insertion point through the text. To edit a document, you must be able to position this insertion point accurately.

   ▶ Press ⎣Home⎦ and ⎣End⎦ a number of times to see how the insertion point moves to the beginning or end of a line.

   ▶ Press ⎣Ctrl⎦+⎣Home⎦ and ⎣Ctrl⎦+⎣End⎦ a number of times to see how the insertion point moves to the beginning or end of the document.

4. Practice using the mouse to point and click to move the insertion point to specific positions.

Completing the Heading

5. Fill out the heading with your name, the filename, and the time and date as shown in this illustration (although your name and the time and date will be different), following these instructions:

   ▶ Move the insertion point to the right end of each line and press ⎣Spacebar⎦ to insert a space, then type in your name and the filename. To enter the current time and date into the document, move the insertion point to where you want it, and then pull down the **Edit** menu and click the **Time/Date** command.

   ▶ If you make mistakes, press ⎣← Bksp⎦ to move the insertion point to the left and delete them.

Enter heading data

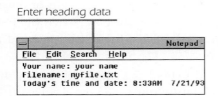

Pressing ⎣Enter↵⎦ with the insertion point at the beginning of the line inserts a blank line.

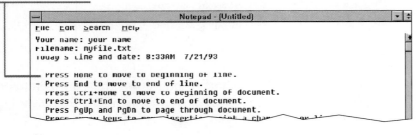

6. Move the insertion point to the very beginning of the first item that begins "- *Press Home*" and press ⎣Enter↵⎦ to enter a blank line between the three-line heading and the rest of the text.

Inserting Text

7. Edit the body of the document by entering the words highlighted in this illustration. To do so, move the insertion point after the space where you want to insert the new words, type the words, and press ⌈Spacebar⌉.

Add these new words.

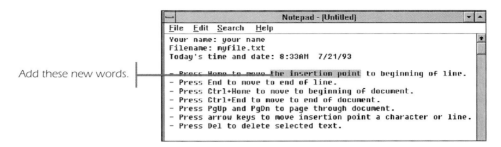

```
─ │                Notepad - [Untitled]              ▼ ▲
 File  Edit  Search  Help
Your name: your name                                      ↑
Filename: myfile.txt
Today's time and date: 8:33AM  7/21/93

- Press Home to move the insertion point to beginning of line.
- Press End to move to end of line.
- Press Ctrl+Home to move to beginning of document.
- Press Ctrl+End to move to end of document.
- Press PgUp and PgDn to page through document.
- Press arrow keys to move insertion point a character or line.
- Press Del to delete selected text.
```

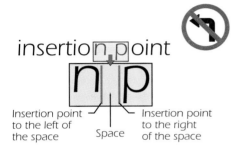

insertio**n** **p**oint

n **p**

Insertion point to the left of the space   Space   Insertion point to the right of the space

COMMON WRONG TURNS: INSERTING TEXT

When you position the insertion point to insert text between two existing words, you can position it on either side of the space that separates the words. If you position it on the left side of the space, you press ⌈Spacebar⌉ before typing the new word. If you position it on the right side of the space, you press ⌈Spacebar⌉ after typing the new word.

Replacing Existing Text

8. Double-click the word *PgUp* to select it.

9. Type **PgDn** and then press ⌈Spacebar⌉ to replace it.

10. Double-click the second *PgDn* on the line to select it.

11. Type **PgUp** and then press ⌈Spacebar⌉ to replace it.

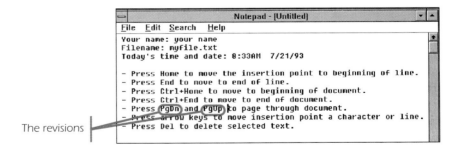

```
─ │                Notepad - [Untitled]              ▼ ▲
 File  Edit  Search  Help
Your name: your name                                      ↑
Filename: myfile.txt
Today's time and date: 8:33AM  7/21/93

- Press Home to move the insertion point to beginning of line.
- Press End to move to end of line.
- Press Ctrl+Home to move to beginning of document.
- Press Ctrl+End to move to end of document.
- Press PgDn and PgUp to page through document.
- Press arrow keys to move insertion point a character or line.
- Press Del to delete selected text.
```

The revisions

Selecting and Deleting Text

12. Point to the left of the hyphen in the last line—the line that reads "*Press Del to delete selected text.*"

13. Hold down the left button and drag the cursor to extend the highlight over the entire sentence including the period at the end of the line.

14. Release the mouse button, and the sentence remains highlighted.

15. Press ⌈Del⌉ to delete the highlighted sentence. Your finished document should now look like the following illustration:

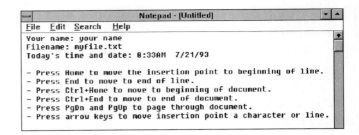

```
┌─────────────────────────────────────────────────────────────┐
│ ─                Notepad - [Untitled]                   ▼ ▲  │
├─────────────────────────────────────────────────────────────┤
│  File  Edit  Search  Help                                    │
├─────────────────────────────────────────────────────────────┤
│ Your name: your name                                     ▲   │
│ Filename: myfile.txt                                         │
│ Today's time and date: 8:33AM  7/21/93                       │
│                                                              │
│ - Press Home to move the insertion point to beginning of line│
│ - Press End to move to end of line.                          │
│ - Press Ctrl+Home to move to beginning of document.          │
│ - Press Ctrl+End to move to end of document.                 │
│ - Press PgDn and PgUp to page through document.              │
│ - Press arrow keys to move insertion point a character or line│
└─────────────────────────────────────────────────────────────┘
```

16. Leave the document on the screen as you read the following section on saving documents and clearing the screen.

PAUSING FOR PRACTICE

Moving the insertion point with the keyboard and mouse pointer and selecting text are basic skills. Continue practicing these procedures until you are comfortable with them.

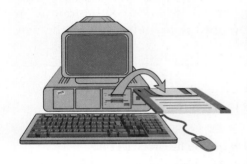

SAVING DOCUMENTS AND CLEARING THE SCREEN

When you create a new file or edit one that you have opened from a disk, it exists only in the computer's memory until you save it. Saving the document copies it from the computer's memory to the disk, where it is permanently stored.

To save a file, you pull down the **File** menu and click the **Save** command. You then fill in the necessary information in the Save As dialog box and click the **OK** command button.

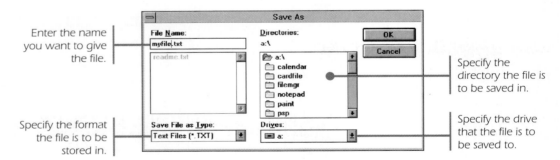

Enter the name you want to give the file.

Specify the format the file is to be stored in.

Specify the directory the file is to be saved in.

Specify the drive that the file is to be saved to.

To save the file in a specific location, it may be necessary to change the drive and directory. To change the drive, click the down arrow on the **Drives** drop-down list box to display a list of the drives on your system. Scroll the drive you want into view and click it to select it. To change the directory, double-click its name in the **Directories** list box. This takes you down into the directory and displays any of the directory's subdirectories in the **Directories** list box and any of its files in the **File Name** window.

The first time you save a document, you have to enter its filename into the **File Name** text box. When you save the file again, you needn't specify the name again unless you want to change it. In that case, you pull down the **File** menu and click the **Save As** command. Remember from PicTorial 3 that with Windows (or DOS), you can assign names to files that have up to eight characters and an extension of up to three characters separated from the name by a period. Most Windows applications assign a unique extension to the files they create so you and the applications can tell which files belong to which applications. Notepad adds the extension *.txt*.

When you are finished with a document and want to work on another, you pull down the **File** menu and click the **New** command to clear the old document from the screen.

▶▶ TUTORIAL

Saving a New File

1. Pull down Notepad's **File** menu and click the **Save** command to display the Save As dialog box. The entry *.txt in the **File Name** text box is highlighted.

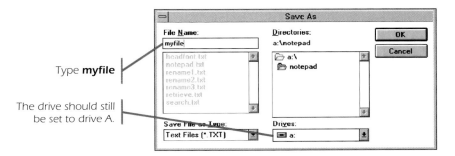

Type **myfile**

The drive should still be set to drive A.

   ▶ Check that drive A is still selected. If it isn't, select it.

   ▶ Check that the *notepad* directory is still selected. If it isn't, select it.

2. Click the **File Name** text box to move the insertion point there, and type **myfile**

3. Click the **OK** command button to save the document.

4. Pull down the **File** menu and click the **New** command to clear the screen.

Opening the Saved File

5. Pull down the **File** menu and click the **Open** command to display the Open dialog box. The path *a:\notepad* below the **Directories** heading indicates that the drive is still set to drive A and the selected directory is still *notepad*.

6. Double-click *myfile.txt* in the list of files to open the file. (The *.txt* extension was added by Notepad when you first saved the file.) The document looks just as it did when you saved it.

Saving a File a Second Time

7. Pull down the **File** menu and click the **Save** command again. This time the file is saved without displaying a dialog box.

Saving a File Under a New Name

8. Pull down the **File** menu and click the **Save As** command to dis-

The original file-
name preceded
by its path.

File Name:
a:\notepad\myfile.txt

file.txt
file1.txt
file10.txt
file11.txt
file2.txt
file3.txt
file4.txt
file5.txt

play the Save As dialog box again. The original filename is high-lighted in the **File Name** text box along with its path.

9. Type **myfile2** and press [Enter←] to save the file under a new name.

Opening the Saved File

10. Pull down the **File** menu and click the **New** command to clear the screen.

11. Pull down the **File** menu and click the **Open** command to display the Open dialog box.

12. Double-click the file *myfile2.txt* in the list of files to open the file. It is an exact copy of the *myfile.txt* file that you saved it from.

PRINTING DOCUMENTS

When you are ready to print a file, almost every Windows application has a **Print Setup** command on the **File** menu. You use this command to specify the printer you want to print on, change the orientation of the document on the page, or change the size and source of the paper to be used.

Click here to use the default printer.

Click here to change printers.

Click here to change the orienta-tion of the docu-ment on the page.

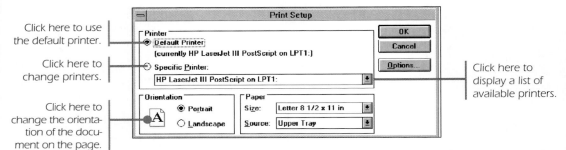

Click here to display a list of available printers.

Orientation refers to portrait or landscape mode. *Portrait mode* prints across the narrow width of the page. *Landscape mode* prints across the length of the page. The terms are taken from the fine arts, where por-traits are usually painted in one orientation and landscapes in the other.

Notepad's **Page Setup** command on the **File** menu gives you some control over your printout. For example, you can change headers, foot-ers, and margins. When you execute this command, the Page Setup dia-log box is displayed. The *&f* in the **Header** text box is a code that prints the filename as a header at the top of every page. The *Page &p* in the **Footer** text box prints the word *Page* followed by the page number as a footer at the bottom of every page. The numbers in the Margin boxes specify the four margins on the printed page.

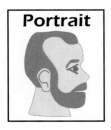

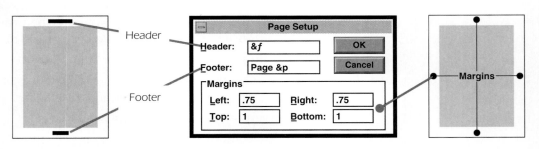

Header

Footer

▶▶ **TUTORIAL**

Getting Started

1. Pull down Notepad's **File** menu and click the **Open** command to display the Open dialog box. The **Drives** box should indicate that the drive is still drive A and the directory is still *notepad*.

2. Click the file *notepad.txt* in the list of files to select it, and then click the **OK** command button to open the document. When the document is opened, the document that was on the screen is automatically cleared.

Changing Margins

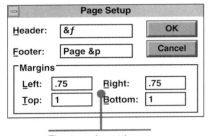

3. Pull down the **File** menu and click the **Page Setup** command to display the Page Setup dialog box. The *&f* code in the **Header** text box is highlighted.

4. Double-click the *.75* in the **Left** Margins box to highlight it, then type **1** to replace it.

The margin settings

5. Press [Tab⇆] to highlight the *.75* in the **Right** Margins box to highlight it, then type **1** to replace it.

6. Click the **OK** command button to complete your changes and return to the document.

Printing the Document

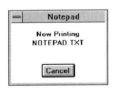

7. Pull down the **File** menu and click the **Print** command to print the document. In a moment a dialog box tells you it is being printed.

Identifying Available Printers

8. Pull down the **File** menu and click the **Print Setup** command to display the Print Setup dialog box.

9. Click the arrow for the drop-down list under the heading **Specific Printer** to list the printers that are available on your system. The name of the current printer is selected. If you have more than one printer listed, write down their names and ask what they are used for.

Click here to display a drop-down list of the printers on your system.

The list of printers is displayed here.

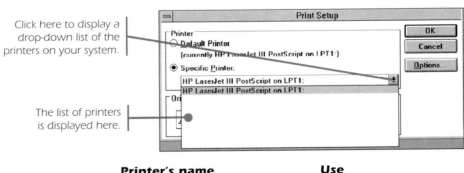

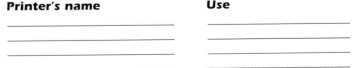

Printer's name	Use
_____	_____
_____	_____
_____	_____
_____	_____

10. Click the **Cancel** command button to close the dialog box without making any changes.

USING PRINT MANAGER

Most documents are eventually printed so a record can be filed or distributed to others. When you print a file from any Windows application, it is first printed to the disk. The file on the disk is then sent to the printer. This is done because a computer can send a file to the disk much faster than it can print it out on most printers. By printing to the disk first, Windows allows you to resume editing while it sends the file on the disk to the printer. This can save you quite a bit of time.

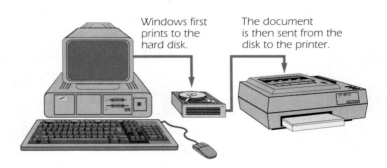

Printing to the disk also allows you to print one document after another without waiting for each to be finished before starting the next one. The lineup of print jobs waiting to be printed is called a *print queue*. When you have such a queue, even if it contains only one print job, Print Manager is opened and its icon appears on the desktop. To cancel or manage jobs in the queue, you double-click the icon to display the Print Manager window.

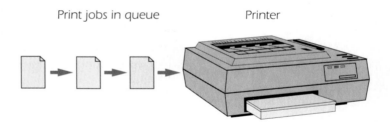

COMMON WRONG TURN: PRINT MANAGER DOESN'T APPEAR

If Print Manager does not appear when you print a document, or if you cannot resume editing until the entire document has finished printing, then Print Manager has been turned off on your system. To turn it back on, open the Main group window and double-click the Control Panel icon to open another window. Double-click the Printers icon to display a dialog box. Click the **Use Print Manager** check box to turn it on, then click the **Close** command button to return to the Control Panel. Finally, minimize or close the Control Panel window.

The Print Manager window contains a menu, command buttons, and a list of printers below each of which are listed the print jobs being processed.

Menu

Command buttons

Printers on the system, with the status of each

Print jobs being processed for the printer

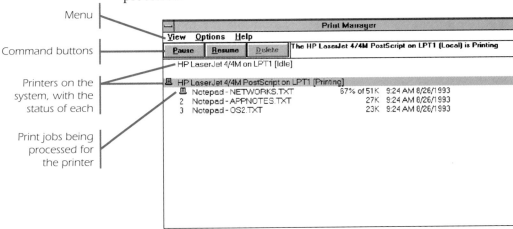

When a job is being printed to the disk, a dialog box keeps you informed of its progress.

If any problem arises, an error message is displayed.

Status of the print job

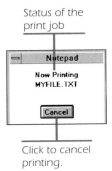

Click to cancel printing.

Fix printer and click.

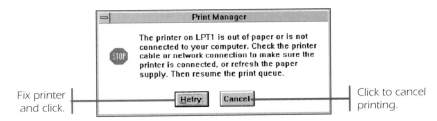

Click to cancel printing.

To manage printers and print jobs, you highlight either the printer or one of the jobs and then choose one of the command buttons.

Pauses the selected printer

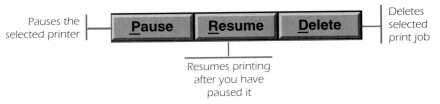

Deletes selected print job

Resumes printing after you have paused it

The **View** menu lists commands that specify what information is displayed by Print Manager.

Displays information about print jobs

Immediately updates the list of jobs waiting to be printed

Displays print queues for network printers

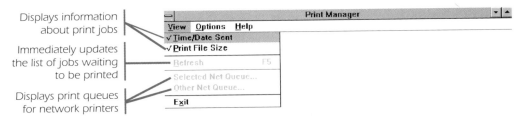

If you close Print Manager before all jobs are printed, a dialog box warns you that print jobs will be canceled.

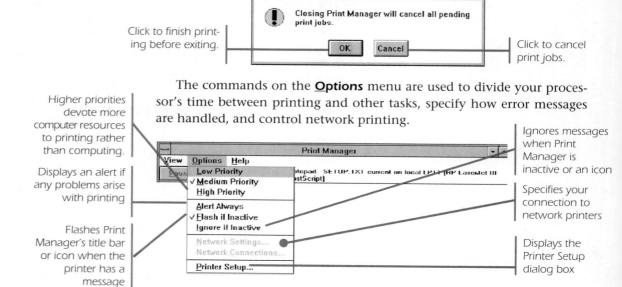

Click to finish printing before exiting.

Click to cancel print jobs.

The commands on the **Options** menu are used to divide your processor's time between printing and other tasks, specify how error messages are handled, and control network printing.

Higher priorities devote more computer resources to printing rather than computing.

Displays an alert if any problems arise with printing

Flashes Print Manager's title bar or icon when the printer has a message

Ignores messages when Print Manager is inactive or an icon

Specifies your connection to network printers

Displays the Printer Setup dialog box

▶▶ TUTORIAL

Getting Ready

1. Insert your *Windows Student Resource Disk* into drive A.

Opening a Document to Print

2. Pull down Notepad's **File** menu and click the **Open** command to display the dialog box you'll see when you open documents with almost all Windows applications.

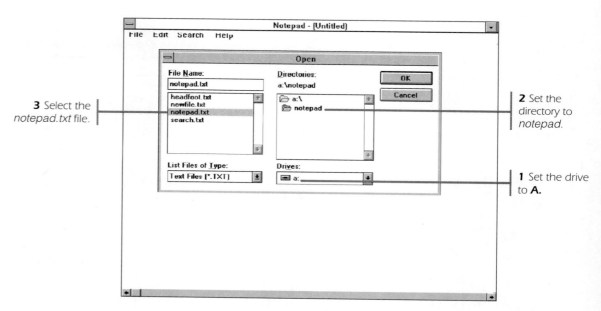

3 Select the *notepad.txt* file.

2 Set the directory to *notepad*.

1 Set the drive to **A**.

3. Open the *notepad.txt* file stored in the *notepad* directory on drive A.

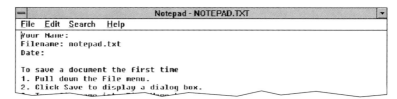

Pausing Print Manager

4. Open Program Manager's Main group window and double-click the Print Manager icon to open the application. (If you can't see the Main group window, you may want to temporarily minimize Notepad so it is displayed as an icon.)

Print Manager

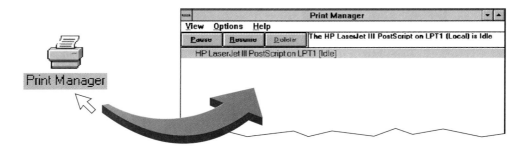

> **COMMON WRONG TURNS:**
> **CAN'T FIND A WINDOW OR ICON**
>
> When you are working on an application, Program Manager may be automatically minimized so it's displayed as an icon or it may be hidden behind the application window. To see Program Manager, minimize the application that is hiding it. To see Program Manager's contents, double-click its icon to open it.

5. Click the name of the printer you are using and then click the **Pause** command button. The name of your printer should be followed by the notice *[Paused]*. Now no jobs will be printed until you decide they should be. This allows you to send a number of jobs to the printer so you can experience working with a print queue.

2 Click to pause the printer.

1 Click to select a printer.

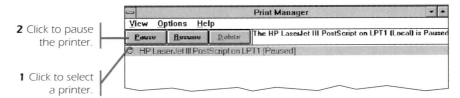

Creating a Print Queue

6. Minimize Print Manager and maximize Notepad.

7. Pull down Notepad's **File** menu and click the **Print** command.

8. Repeat Step 7 five more times to send a total of six printouts to the printer.

9. Minimize Notepad and Maximize Print Manager. All six print jobs are listed under the heading for your printer.

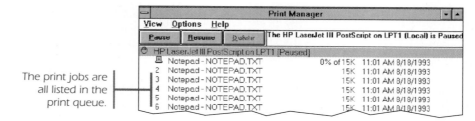

The print jobs are all listed in the print queue.

Deleting Jobs

10. Highlight the last job in the print queue and click the **Delete** command button to display a dialog box asking you to confirm the deletion.

2 Click this command button to delete the selected file.

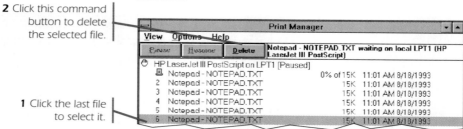

1 Click the last file to select it.

11. Click the **OK** command button to delete the job from the print queue

12. Repeat Steps 10 and 11 until all but one of the print jobs have been canceled.

Resuming the Printer

13. Click the name of the printer you are using to select it, then click the **Resume** command button. The *[Paused]* message disappears, and the last document prints.

14. Click the Print Manager's Minimize button to run it as an icon on the desktop.

USING THE CLIPBOARD TO COPY AND MOVE TEXT

Notepad, like most other applications, makes it easy for you to copy or move data in a document. To do so, you first select the data you want to copy or move, then copy or cut the selected data, and then paste it back in elsewhere in the document.

When you copy or move data, you are using Windows' Clipboard. The data that you copy or cut is first copied or moved to the Clipboard, where it remains until you copy or cut other data or exit Windows. While the data is stored on the Clipboard, you can paste it anywhere in the document you copied or cut it from. You can also paste it into another document, or even into another application's document.

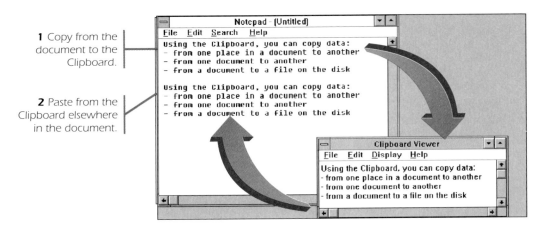

1 Copy from the document to the Clipboard.

2 Paste from the Clipboard elsewhere in the document.

COPYING OR CUTTING TO THE CLIPBOARD

You can copy or cut two types of information to the Clipboard: data or graphics. Data consists of letters and numbers like those you enter to write a letter or calculate a loan. The data can be edited and revised once you paste it into another application.

To copy or cut data onto the Clipboard, use one of these procedures:

▶ To copy or cut data from an application, select the data, then pull down the application's **Edit** menu and click the **Copy** or **Cut** command. **Copy** leaves the original data intact and makes a copy of it on the Clipboard. **Cut** removes the original data from the application's file and transfers it to the Clipboard.

▶ To copy a snapshot (bitmap) of the entire screen to the Clipboard, press [PrtScr]. (This only works in *386 enhanced mode*.) If this doesn't work on your system, try holding down [Alt] or [⇧ Shift] while you press [PrtScr] since pressing [PrtScr] by itself does not work on some systems. (The graphics that you capture this way are called bitmaps because they are made up of light or dark bits arranged in a grid. These graphics are assigned the extension *.bmp* when you save them and can be pasted only into some types of applications.)

▶ To copy a snapshot (bitmap) of just the active window to the Clipboard, press [Alt]+[PrtScr]. If this doesn't work on your system, try holding down [⇧ Shift] while you press [PrtScr].

Viewing Data on the Clipboard

To see what is on the Clipboard, double-click the Clipboard icon to open the Viewer. The Clipboard Viewer's menu lists a number of menu names.

▶ Pull down the **File** menu to open and save the Clipboard file or to exit the Viewer. (You save the contents of the Clipboard when you want to have access to it again. The saved file has the extension *.clp*.)

▶ Pull down the **Edit** menu and click the **Delete** command to delete the contents of the Clipboard.

▶ Pull down the **Display** menu when you want to change the way data are displayed.

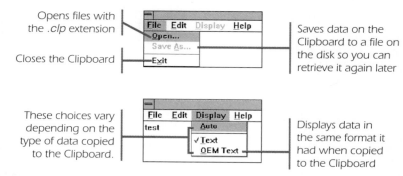

Opens files with the .*clp* extension

Closes the Clipboard

Saves data on the Clipboard to a file on the disk so you can retrieve it again later

These choices vary depending on the type of data copied to the Clipboard.

Displays data in the same format it had when copied to the Clipboard

Pasting Data from the Clipboard

To paste data from the Clipboard, move the insertion point to where you want it pasted, pull down the **Edit** menu, and click the **Paste** command.

▶▶ TUTORIAL

Getting Ready

1. Use Notepad to open the *search.txt* file stored in the *notepad* directory on the *Windows Student Resource Disk* on drive A.

2. Select the entire line that reads *Examples of case* (scroll or maximize the window to see it). To do so, point to the left of the *E* in *Examples,* hold down the left mouse button, and drag the mouse down to the blank line below the paragraph, then release the mouse button.

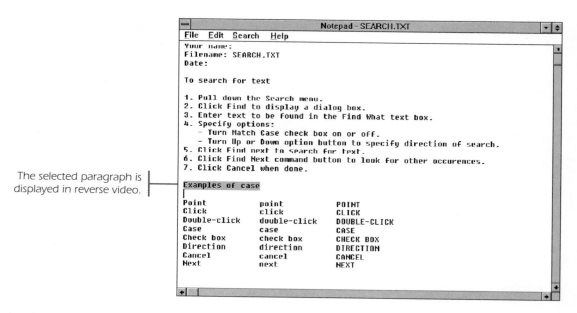

The selected paragraph is displayed in reverse video.

Moving Text

3. Pull down the **Edit** menu and click the **Cut** command to move the paragraph from the document to the Clipboard.

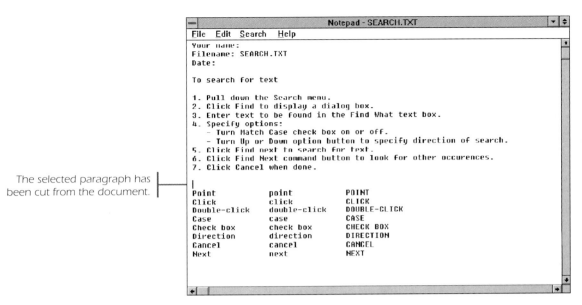

The selected paragraph has been cut from the document.

4. Press Ctrl+End to move the insertion point to the end of the document, and press Enter← twice to move the insertion point down two lines.

5. Pull down the **Edit** menu and click the **Paste** command to copy the paragraph from the Clipboard back into the document.

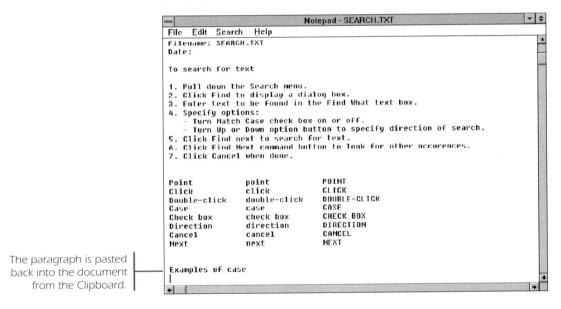

The paragraph is pasted back into the document from the Clipboard.

Copying Text

6. Select the same line of text again (in its new position) just as you did in Step 2.

7. Pull down the **Edit** menu and click the **Copy** command to copy the paragraph from the document to the Clipboard.

8. Move the insertion point to the first blank line above the three columns of terms.

9. Pull down the **Edit** menu and click the **Paste** command to copy the paragraph from the Clipboard back into the document. You now have two copies of the same paragraph.

10. Print the document.

Viewing Data on the Clipboard

11. Open the Main group and double-click the Clipboard Viewer icon to open it. Click the window's Maximize button to enlarge it. The line of text that you just copied is on the Clipboard.

Clipboard Viewer

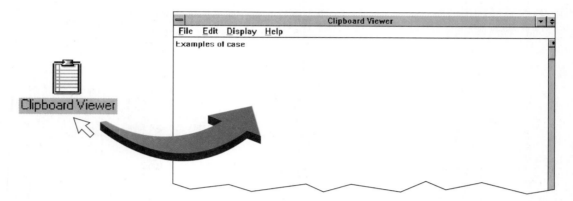

12. Press PrtScr, and the image of the screen is copied to the Clipboard.

PAUSING FOR PRACTICE

Cutting, copying, and pasting text are basic skills in almost all Windows applications. Pause here to practice these procedures until you have mastered them. You will not be saving the file when you are finished, so feel free to copy, move, and delete any text.

Finishing Up

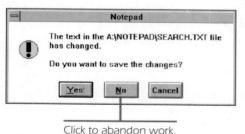

Click to abandon work.

13. Double-click the Clipboard Viewer's Control-menu box (the top-most one) to close the application.

14. Double-click the Notepad's Control-menu box to close the application. Since you have not saved your changes, a dialog box appears warning you.

15. Click the **No** command button because you don't want to save the changes.

▶▶ **SKILL-BUILDING EXERCISES**

1. **Retrieving Documents with Notepad**

Windows supplies a number of files with the extension *.txt* that you can open with Notepad. These files are normally stored in the Windows directory (usually on drive C). Open some of these files with Notepad and make a printout of at least one of them.

2. **Creating a Time-Log Document**

1. Clear the Notepad window and type **.LOG** in the upper-left corner (it must be all uppercase).

2. Save the document in the *notepad* directory on your *Windows Student Resource Disk* in drive A as *timelog.txt*.

3. Clear the screen and then open *timelog.txt*. You'll see that the time and date have automatically been entered.

4. Type the sentence **This is my first log entry**, then save the file again and clear the screen.

5. Open the file again, and you'll see that a new time and date have been entered. You can use this document to keep track of activities, since the time and date are updated each time you open the file.

6. Print the document.

3. Exploring Notepad's Help

Explore Notepad's on-line help. You'll find definitions of such terms as *text files*, *headers*, and *footers*. You'll also find summaries of many of the procedures you have just completed.

4. Revising Headers and Footers

1. Use Notepad to open the *headfoot.txt* document supplied in the *notepad* directory on the *Windows Student Resource Disk*.

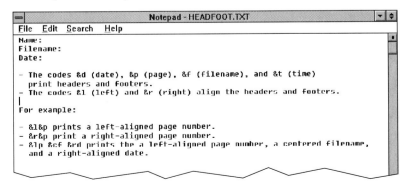

2. Before printing the document, use the Page Setup command to change the header and footer using one or more of the codes listed shown here. Experiment with these codes to change the alignment of your headers and footers. Keep in mind that you can use these codes in combinations.

5. Copying Text

1. Open the *search.txt* document supplied in the *notepad* directory on the *Windows Student Resource Disk* and make a duplicate copy of each line in the 3-line heading.

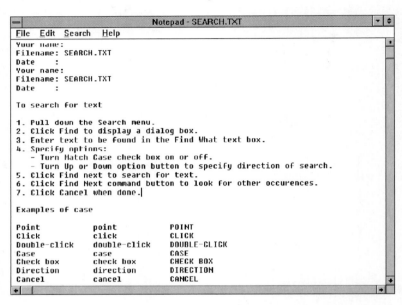

2. Reorganize the examples at the bottom of the document into ascending alphabetical order.

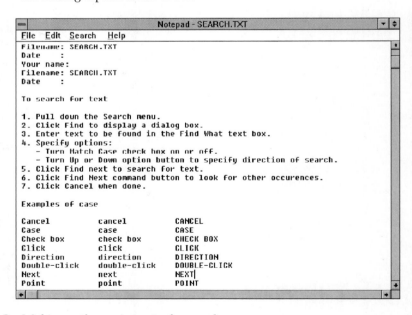

3. Make another printout of your changes.

4. Clear the screen without saving your changes.

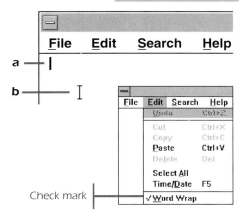

File   Edit   Search   Help

a —— |

b —— I

Check mark

File Edit Search Help
Undo   Ctrl+Z
Cut   Ctrl+X
Copy   Ctrl+C
Paste   Ctrl+V
Delete   Del
Select All
Time/Date   F5
√ Word Wrap

1. This illustration shows two elements that appear on the Notepad screen. What is the name of each?

a. _____

b. _____

2. Describe what happens as you enter text when the check mark is in front of the **Word Wrap** command and when it isn't.

When it is: _____

When it isn't: _____

3. This illustration shows the dialog box that appears when you pull down the **File** menu and choose the **Open** command on almost all Windows applications. Describe what each element shows.

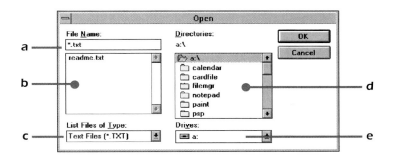

a. _____

b. _____

c. _____

d. _____

e. _____

4. This illustration shows the dialog box that appears when you pull down the **File** menu and choose the **Save** command on almost all Windows applications. Describe what each element shows.

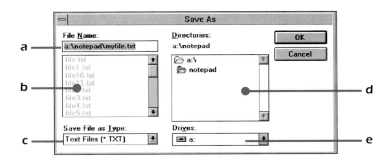

a. _____

b. _____

c. _____

d. _____

e. _____

5. This illustration shows the dialog box that appears when you pull down the **File** menu and choose the **Print Setup** command on almost all Windows applications. Describe what each element shows.

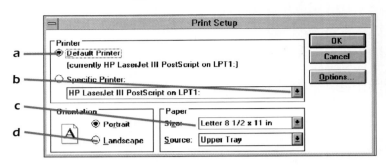

a. _____

b. _____

c. _____

d. _____

6. Describe how you would select the sections of text shown here.

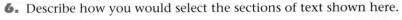

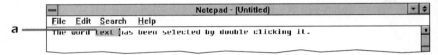

a. _____

b. _____

7. Assuming the insertion point is located where shown in this illustration, list the key or keys you would press to move it to each of the indicated positions.

a. _____

b. _____

c. _____

d. _____

8. Assuming the insertion point is located where shown in this illustration, list the key you would press to delete:

the word *can* _____
the word *text* _____

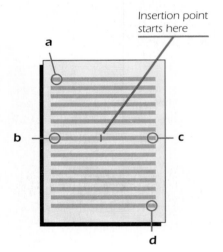

Insertion point starts here

PicTorial 6

Using DOS Applications

After completing this topic, you will be able to:

▶ Display the DOS command prompt without leaving Windows

▶ Run non-Windows applications

Windows runs on top of the DOS operating system, which must be loaded before Windows is loaded. You can access the DOS command prompt without leaving Windows, and you can run non-Windows applications (those designed to run under DOS and not Windows) within Windows.

UNDERSTANDING STANDARD AND ENHANCED MODES

Windows has been designed to take advantage of features available only on high-end PCs. At the same time, however, it can run on less powerful computers. The way it does this is by switching *modes,* or methods of operation. On more powerful computers (those with 386, 486, or Pentium processors) Windows runs in *enhanced mode.* On less powerful computers, Windows runs in *standard mode.* The difference between these two modes is significant. For example, in enhanced mode, you can run non-Windows applications in windows. In standard mode you can't—they can only be run full screen. In enhanced mode, Windows stores parts of large active programs and files on the hard disk until it needs them. In a way this makes the space on the disk act as if it were part of the computer's internal random access memory, or RAM. In standard mode, Windows can't do this, so you can't work on applications or data files that are as large.

To see what mode your system is using, pull down Program Manager's **Help** menu and click the **About Program Manager** command. A dialog box tells you what mode your system is running in. Click the **OK** command button to close the dialog box.

▶▶ **TUTORIAL**

1. Display Program Manager.

2. Pull down the **Help** menu and click the **About Program Manager** command to display a dialog box that tells you what mode your system is in. Note the mode.

The system's mode ———

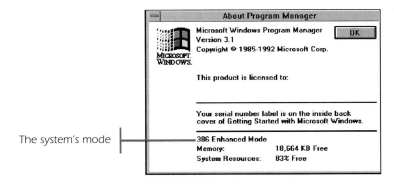

3. Click the **OK** command button to close the dialog box.

ACCESSING AND EXITING THE DOS COMMAND PROMPT

Any time you are using Windows, you can access the DOS command prompt to run DOS applications or use DOS commands that are not available on File Manager's menus.

To display the DOS command prompt, double-click the DOS icon in the Main or Accessories group window. When you double-click the DOS icon, the DOS command prompt is displayed.

If your system is running in enhanced mode, you can press `Alt`+`Enter ←` to run DOS in a window, or if it is running in a window, press `Alt`+`Enter ←` to run it full screen. When DOS is displayed in a window, you can use the window's Minimize and Maximize buttons just as you do on any other window.

To exit DOS, type **exit** and press `Enter ←`. You can't exit Windows without first exiting DOS. If you try to, you'll get an error message.

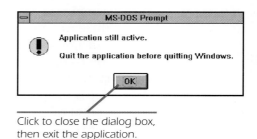

Click to close the dialog box, then exit the application.

TIP: FORGETTING THAT WINDOWS IS STILL RUNNING

It's not unusual to access the DOS prompt from Windows and then forget that Windows is still loaded. If you do forget and turn off the computer without first returning to Windows and exiting it correctly, you can lose work. To have the DOS command prompt remind you that Windows is still loaded, add a line such as *SET WINPMT=Type Exit and press Enter to return to Windows $_$_PG* to your *autoexec.bat* file.

▶▶ TUTORIAL

1. Open the Main group window and double-click the DOS icon to display the DOS command prompt. (Your DOS icon may be different from the one shown here and if the Windows on your system was upgraded from an earlier version, the DOS icon may be in the Accessories group window.)

MS-DOS Prompt

2. Insert your *Windows Student Resource Disk* into drive A.

3. If your system is running in enhanced mode, press Alt + Enter↵ to display DOS in a window. Otherwise, skip to Step 5.

4. Press Alt + Enter↵ again to display DOS full screen.

PAUSING FOR PRACTICE

Switching DOS applications back and forth between full-screen and windowed operation is a basic skill. Continue pressing Alt + Enter↵ a few times to switch back and forth between running DOS full screen and running it in a window.

5. Type **a:** and press Enter↵ to change the default drive to drive A.

6. Type **dir** and press Enter↵ to display a directory of the files on your disk.

7. Type **exit** and press Enter← to end your DOS session and return to Windows. If DOS was running in a window, its window closes automatically.

USING NON-WINDOWS APPLICATIONS

There are times when you want to stay in Windows to use an application designed to run with DOS but not with Windows. The DOS versions of Lotus 1-2-3 and WordPerfect are widely used examples of these *non-Windows applications*. To open a non-Windows application, you can add its icon to one of Program Manager's group windows and double-click it just as you do with Windows applications. However, if the application has not been added to a group window, you can open it in a number of other ways. You can:

▶ Double-click the application's executable program filename in File Manager's contents list. For example, to load WordPerfect, double-click the file named *wp.exe*.

▶ Use the **Run** command located on Program Manager's **File** menu. This command displays a dialog box into which you can type the path and filename of the executable program file that starts the application. Alternatively, you can click the dialog box's **Browse** command button and then browse through directories on your disks to locate the desired file.

▶ Access the DOS command prompt and type the application's path and executable program filename.

Enter the path and executable filename of the program you want to run.

[Run dialog box image]

Run
Command Line:
☐ Run Minimized
OK
Cancel
Browse...
Help

Turn on to have the application open as an icon instead of a window.

Click to browse through directories for the file you want to run.

TIP: EXECUTABLE FILES

If you use File Manager to look in a directory containing one of your applications, you will see many filenames. However, only one of the files is the one you load to open the application. This file is an *executable program file* and almost always ends with the extension *.exe* or *.com*. For example, the executable program file for Windows is *win.com* and for Write it is *write.exe*. To start such a program, you double-click the executable program file's name or you pull down the **File** menu, click the **Run** command, type the filename (not including the extension), and press Enter←.

Once the application is running, you can press Alt + Enter← to switch back and forth between running it in a window or running it full screen if your system is running in enhanced mode. When a non-Windows application is running in a window, it takes up more memory and may operate more slowly, but you can click its Minimize button to run it as an icon, drag and resize its window (within limits), and otherwise treat it much like a Windows application.

To close a non-Windows application, you must first exit it using its own exit command. This removes the application from the computer's memory and removes its display or icon from the desktop. If you try to exit Windows without first exiting an open non-Windows application, a warning is displayed.

If you are running a non-Windows application and it misbehaves, you may find that you can't exit it in the normal way. If this happens, click the window's Control-menu box to display the Control menu. Click the **Se_ttings** command, and then click the **Terminate** command button. Be careful with this command and use it only as a last resort, since it is similar to a local reboot and you could lose data. If you can't display the Control menu, you can still press [Ctrl]+[Alt]+[Del] and follow the instructions displayed on the screen to exit the application.

▶▶ TUTORIAL

Getting Ready

1. To load a DOS application, you must first know its name and where it is located on your system. In this section, we'll load an application called QBASIC (or BASIC or BASICA on DOS 4 and earlier versions) that is stored in the DOS directory on drive C. If your instructor wants you to load another application, he or she will supply you with the following information:

Question	Example	Your Information
Name of application:	Microsoft QBASIC	_____
Name of its executable file:	*qbasic.exe*	_____
Path to the executable file:	*c:\dos*	_____
Command you use to exit the application:	[Alt]+[F], [X]	_____

Loading a DOS Application Using the Browse Command

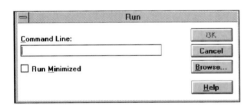

2. Pull down Program Manager's **File** menu and click the **Run** command to display a dialog box.

3. Click the **Browse** command button to display the Browse dialog box. This box is identical to the Open dialog box that you use to open documents.

4. Make these settings:

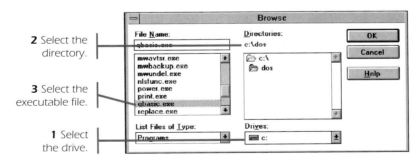

2 Select the directory.

3 Select the executable file.

1 Select the drive.

▶ Select the drive and directory where your DOS files are located. For example, select drive C in the **Dri_ves** drop-down box, then the *dos* directory in the **Directories** box. This will display a list of the files in that directory in the **File _Name** box.

▶ Select the name of the executable file that runs your application. For QBASIC, scroll the *qbasic.exe* filename into view and click it to select it.

COMMON WRONG TURNS: CAN'T FIND A DIRECTORY

When you use the **Browse** command, it may display a dialog box for a directory other than the one you want. Often you have to move up to the root directory to find the directory you are looking for. For example, clicking the **Browse** command button may display the files in the *c:\windows* directory. To see the files in the *c:\dos* directory you have to first double-click *c:* in the **Directories** box to move up to the root directory and then double-click the *dos* directory. Be sure to check the path listed under the heading **Directories** to be sure of your current location.

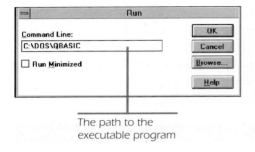

The path to the executable program

5. Click the **OK** command button to return to the Run dialog box.

6. Click the **OK** command button to run the selected application.

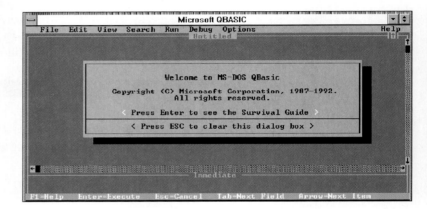

7. If you loaded QBASIC, press Esc to clear the opening screen.

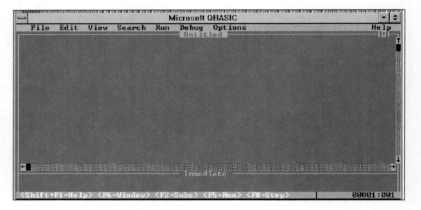

8. If the application is displayed in a window, press Alt+Enter↵ to display it at full screen.

Closing a DOS Application

9. If you loaded QBASIC, press Alt+ F to pull down the **File** menu, then press X to exit the application and return to Windows. If you loaded another application, use its exit command instead. When you exit the application, it is no longer displayed on the desktop.

Loading a DOS Application by Typing Its Name

10. Pull down Program Manager's **File** menu and click the **Run** command to display a dialog box.

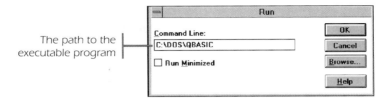

The path to the executable program

11. Type **c:\dos\qbasic** (or the path and application name you are using) and click the **OK** command button to load the application. This method of loading a application is faster if you know the executable file's exact name and path.

Finishing Up

12. If you loaded QBASIC again, press [Esc] to clear the opening screen. Then exit the program as you did in Step 9. If you loaded another application, use its exit command instead.

▶▶ SKILL-BUILDING EXERCISES

1. Running DOS Programs

1. Ask your instructor for the names of other executable program files that are on your system and enter information about them in the spaces provided.

Question	Program 1	Program 2
Name of application	_____	_____
Name of its executable program file	_____	_____
Path to the executable program file	_____	_____
Command you use to exit the program	_____	_____

2. Run each of these applications and then exit them.

PicTorial 6 ▶VISUALQUIZ

1. Explain how you display the DOS command prompt shown here without leaving Windows.

How do you then return to Windows?

---

2. What keys do you press to run DOS in a window like this?

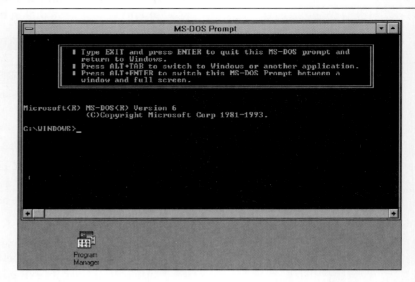

What mode does your system have to be in when you do so?

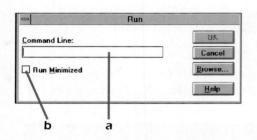

3. What command would you enter in the **Command Line** text box (a) to run a program in the directory named *lotus* on drive C that you normally loaded by typing **123** from the DOS command prompt? What would be the result of turning on the **Run Minimized** check box (b)?

a. _____

b. _____

True-False (Circle T if the statement is true or F if it is false.)

T F **1.** When you use a Windows application to create a file containing data, the file is referred to as a *document*.

T F **2.** To start an application, you click its icon.

T F **3.** When you have finished working with Windows for the day, just turn it off and everything will automatically take care of itself.

T F **4.** When working on a Notepad document, double-clicking in the text selects the entire paragraph.

T F **5.** When you save a document the first time, its name can be only 8 characters long but you can use any of the characters that you can type on the keyboard.

T F **6.** Windows applications assign their own file extensions to files so you can tell which application created which file.

T F **7.** Many printers can print in either portrait or landscape orientation. Portrait orientation is the one we are most familiar with since it is used for letters, reports, and most other documents.

T F **8.** When you use a Windows application to print a document, it is normally printed to the disk before it is sent to the printer.

T F **9.** When you print documents, you must wait until each is finished printing before you start the next.

T F **10.** The lineup of jobs waiting to be printed is called a *cue*.

T F **11.** When you cut or copy data in a document, it is automatically moved or copied to the Clipboard.

T F **12.** Once data is on the Clipboard, it remains there until you exit Windows.

T F **13.** Once data is on the Clipboard, you can paste it into either the current application or another application.

T F **14.** To see what data is on the Clipboard, double-click the Clipboard icon to open the Clipboard Viewer.

T F **15.** You can tell what mode your system is running in by pulling down Program Manager's Help menu and clicking the **About Program Manager** command.

T F **16.** In standard mode, you can run DOS applications in windows and full screen.

T F **17.** To display the DOS command prompt, you must always first exit Windows.

T F **18.** If you display the DOS command prompt without exiting Windows, you return to Windows by typing **quit** and pressing Enter ← .

Multiple Choice (Circle the correct answer.)

1. To open an application program, you ___.

   a. Click its icon

   b. Click its icon and then pull down the **File** menu and click the **Run** command

   c. Double-click its icon

   d. Click its icon and then pull down the **File** menu and click the **Open** command

2. To close or exit an application properly, you ___.

   a. Click its Minimize button

   b. Double-click its Control-menu box

   c. Turn off the computer

   d. Pull down Program Manager's **File** menu and click the **Exit** command

3. To open an existing file, you must know ___.

   a. Its name and the drive it's on

   b. How large it is

   c. The date and time it was created

   d. What characters are legal in filenames

4. To save a file the first time, you must assign it a filename that ___.

   a. Contains 10 or fewer characters in the name and 3 in the extension

   b. Contains only the characters *a* through *z* in lowercase

   c. Contains 8 or fewer legal characters in the name

   d. Can be easily remembered

5. Print Manager appears on the desktop whenever you print a document so you can ___.

   a. Change the quality of the printout

   b. Specify which pages to print

   c. Pause the printer or delete a print job

   d. Add pages numbers to the document

6. Once you have copied data to the Clipboard, you can ___.

   a. Copy it into another document

   b. Move it elsewhere in the same document

   c. Save it into a file on the disk

   d. All of the above

7. To switch back and forth between running a non-Windows application in a window and running it full screen, you ___.

   a. Press [Alt]-[Enter ↵]

   b. Pull down the **Window** menu and click the **Refresh** command

   c. Press [Ctrl]-[Enter ↵]

   d. None of the above

8. To run a non-Windows application, you ___.

    a. Double-click the application's executable program filename in File Manager's contents list

    b. Use the **Run** command located on Program Manager's **File** menu

    c. Access the DOS command prompt and type the application's executable program filename

    d. Any of the above

Fill In the Blank (Enter your answer in the space provided.)

1. To start an application, you _____ its icon.

2. To quickly close an application, you double-click its _____.

3. To open a document, you pull down the **File** menu and click the **Open** command to display a dialog box. You then select a _____ so the names of the files are displayed, select one of the _____, and then click the _____ command button.

4. To save a document the first time, you pull down the **File** menu and click the **Save** command to display a dialog box. You then select a _____, type a _____, and then click the _____ command button.

5. Filenames can have a name of up to _____ characters followed by a _____ and up to _____ more characters.

6. Normally letters are printed in _____ orientation with text printed across the narrow width of the paper.

7. When more than one job is waiting to be printed, it is called a print _____.

8. When you copy or cut data in any Windows application, it is copied or moved to the _____.

9. Data on the Clipboard can be _____ elsewhere in the document.

10. To see the data on the Clipboard, you double-click the _____ icon to display the _____.

11. Windows can only run DOS in a window when it is running in _____ mode. To switch back and forth between running it in a window and running it full screen, press _____.

12. If you double-click the DOS icon to access the DOS command prompt, you return to Windows by typing _____ and then pressing _____.

13. When you try to exit Windows while a DOS application is still running, a _____ is displayed. You must then _____ the application before exiting.

Projects

Project 1. Adding a DOS Application to the Applications Group

In Exercise 1 of PicTorial 6 you gathered information about DOS programs on your system. Use this information to add one of these programs to Program Manager's Applications group. Run the program and exit it, then remove it from the Applications group.

INDEX

About File Manager command, 81
About Program Manager command, 29, 30
Accessories group window, 13
    clock application, 43-44
Active window, 14-15
Adjacent files, selecting by clicking, 92-93
All files:
    selecting by clicking, 92
    selecting with menu, 93
Anxiety, computer, 3
Application icons, 13
Application programs:
    defined, 1
    examples of, 1
    running as icons, 119
    starting/exiting, 118-20
    switching among, 2
Application window, 13
    reducing to an icon, 20
Arrange Icons command, **Window** menu, 43, 79
ASCII text files, 121
Asterisk (*) wildcard, 74
Available printers, identifying, 131

Back command, **Help** menu, 35-36
.bak extension, 71
BASIC, 149
BASICA, 149
.bat extension, 67
.bmp extension, 67
Booting the system, 3-4
    from a floppy disk, 87
Browse command, loading DOS applications using, 149-50
By File Type command, 68

Cancel command, 39
Canceling, print jobs, 132
Cascade command, 43, 79, 80-81, 99
Cascaded windows, 43, 79, 80-81
    defined, 41
Changing:
    directories, 63-64
    directory window display, 75-78
    drive, 60-61
    font, 77-78
    margins, 124, 131
Check boxes, 38
Clicking, 7-9, 22
    opening/closing directories by, 65-66
Clipboard, 136-40
    contents of:
        losing, 159
        copying/cutting text to, 137-38

pasting data from, 138
Viewer, 137, 140
viewing data on, 137, 140
Clock application, 43-44
Closing:
    DOS applications, 150
    File Manager, 59
    multiple directory windows, 79
.clp extension, 67
Cold boot, 4
Collapse Branch command, 66
Collapsing directory levels, 65
.com extension, 67
Command buttons, 18, 30, 34, 38
Commands, canceling, 39
Computer, turning off, 21
Computer anxiety, 3
Computer literacy, defined, 2
Confirmation:
    turning on/off, 95-96
Contents list, 59, 60, 67-68
    selecting files from, 91-95
    updating, 106
Control-menu boxes, 6, 31-33
Control menus, 30-33
    Close command, 59
Copying:
    disks, 88-90
    text, 139-40, 142
Creating:
    directories, 101-4
    subdirectories, 103
Ctr+Alt+Del, 4

Deleting:
    directories, 104-6
    group windows
    print jobs, 136
    text, 127-28
Desktop, 5
    arranging windows and icons on, 41-43
    saving layout of, 41
Destination, 96
Dialog boxes, 37-40
    check boxes, 38
    command buttons, 38
    list boxes, 37-38
    option buttons, 38
    text boxes, 37
Directories:
    changing, 63-64, 122
    creating, 101-4
    deleting, 104-6
    opening/closing:
        by clicking, 65-66
        using the **Tree** menu, 66
    searching, 107-8
    specifying, 122
Directory levels, expanding/collapsing, 65

Directory path, 59, 96
Directory tree, 59, 60, 63, 82
Directory window, 58-59, 62, 75
    closing, 81
    new, opening, 62, 79
    See also Multiple directory windows
Directory window display, changing, 75-78
Disk menu, File Manager, 86-87
    Copy Disk command, 88-89
    Format Disk command, 86, 87
    Label Disk command, 87
    Make System Disk check box, 87
    Network Connections command, 61
    Quick Format check box, 87
    Select Drive command, 61
Disks:
    copying, 88-90
    formatting, 86-88
    labeling, 87, 90-91
    write-protecting, 89
Documents, Notepad:
    entering/editing, 124-28
    moving around, 124, 126
    opening, 123, 134, 140
    printing, 128-31
DOS 6, and Windows program, 13
DOS applications:
    closing, 150
    loading by typing its name, 151
    loading using **Browse** command, 149-50
DOS command prompt, accessing/exiting, 146-48
Double-clicking, 7-9, 22
Double-density disks, 86
Dragging:
    icons, 14-16
    windows, 14-18
Dragging and dropping:
    defined, 99
    and Shift and Ctrl keys, 100
Drive:
    changing, 60-61, 122
    specifying, 122
Drive icons, 59, 60
    selecting, 60-61

Edit menu, Notepad:
    Select All command, 125
    Time/Date command, 126
    Word Wrap command, 126
Enhanced mode, 145
Error messages:
    Print Manager, 133
    There is no disk in drive A, 61
Executable program files, 148
.exe extension, 67, 148
Exit Windows command, 20
Expand All command, 66
Expand Branch command, 66